WILLIAM McKINLEY

PRESIDENTIAL ✦ LEADERS

WILLIAM McKINLEY

LAURA B. EDGE

TFCB

TWENTY-FIRST CENTURY BOOKS/MINNEAPOLIS

For Pat, my mom, and in memory of Frank, my dad

Twenty-First Century Books
A division of Lerner Publishing Group
241 First Avenue North
Minneapolis, MN 55401 U.S.A.

Website address: www.lernerbooks.com

Library of Congress Cataloging-in-Publication Data

Edge, Laura Bufano, 1953–
  William McKinley / by Laura B. Edge.
    p.   cm. — (Presidential leaders)
  Includes bibliographical references and index.
  ISBN-13: 978–0–8225–1508–1 (lib. bdg. : alk. paper)
  ISBN-10: 0–8225–1508–3 (lib. bdg. : alk. paper)
   1. McKinley, William, 1843–1901—Juvenile literature. 2. Presidents—United States—
Biography—Juvenile literature. I. Title. II. Series.
  E711.6.E23 2007
  973.8'8092-dc22
                                           2006008296

Manufactured in the United States of America
1 2 3 4 5 6 – JR – 12 11 10 09 08 07

CONTENTS

In Buffalo, New York, people wait in line outside the Temple of Music to shake hands with President McKinley on September 6, 1901.

INTRODUCTION

*Let us ever remember that our
interest is in concord, not conflict; and
that our real eminence rests in the
victories of peace, not those of war.*
—William McKinley, speech delivered at
Pan-American Exposition, Buffalo, New York

On September 6, 1901, President William McKinley stepped from his carriage in front of the Temple of Music. He was at the Pan-American Exposition—a fair that featured the latest American inventions and technology—in Buffalo, New York. He smiled, waved to the cheering crowd, and walked briskly into the auditorium. A brawny man with a barrel chest and broad shoulders, the president wore pin-striped trousers, a dark frock coat, and a black satin hat. His bushy eyebrows framed deeply set blue-gray eyes. The president looked every bit the statesman.

Wooden chairs in the Temple of Music had been arranged to form a wide aisle for a receiving line for the president. McKinley stood under a U.S. flag, flanked by potted palms. John Milburn, the president of the exposition, stood at his left side. McKinley's secretary, George Cortelyou, stood on his right. Well-wishers entered the auditorium from the east, passed a raised platform where the president stood, and exited to the south. Soldiers, police officers, and secret service agents (the president's security team) scattered throughout the auditorium and watched the crowd carefully. A song by J. S. Bach floated from the temple's pipe organ, the largest organ in the world.

Cortelyou looked at his watch impatiently. In precisely ten minutes, he would close the doors, signaling the end of the reception. Men, women, and children filed past the president and shook his hand. Many paused to wipe the sweat off their foreheads with handkerchiefs. The heat was sweltering. At 4:07 P.M., Leon Czolgosz, a short, slender young man wearing a dark gray suit, reached McKinley. A white handkerchief covered his right hand. McKinley, thinking the man's right hand was injured, smiled and reached out to shake his left hand. Czolgosz shoved McKinley's hand away and fired two shots from a .32-caliber short-barreled revolver into the president.

As friends helped McKinley to a nearby chair, the president saw secret service agents wrestling his attacker to the ground. "Don't let them hurt him," he commanded. The crowd broke out in a panic and stampeded toward the door. McKinley held his stomach and then lifted a bloody hand to his secretary. "My wife," he whispered, "be careful, Cortelyou, how you tell her, oh, be careful!"

An experimental electric-powered ambulance carried the president to a small hospital on the exposition grounds. One bullet had grazed his ribs. It fell out of his clothing as the doctors prepared him for surgery. The other bullet had torn through the president's stomach and lodged inside his abdomen. The doctors stitched the holes in McKinley's stomach, but they could not find the second bullet. (Had they thought of it, they might have used a new invention on display at the exhibition, Thomas Edison's x-ray machine, to locate the bullet.) After surgery, McKinley's doctors took him to John Milburn's home, where McKinley's wife, Ida, waited.

News of the attack spread across the shocked nation. Vice President Theodore Roosevelt and other government officials rushed to Buffalo. The press set up several tents across the street from the president's sickbed, and reporters milled about waiting for the latest reports on McKinley's condition. Newspapers printed extra editions every few hours. People around the country prayed for their fallen leader and waited to see if he would recover. Most expressed stunned disbelief that their kind and gentle president could be the target of an assassin's bullet. The waiting was especially hard on folks in Ohio, where the president had been born.

CHAPTER ONE

A GOOD, STEADY YOUNG FELLOW

He was just like other boys, except that he was of a more serious turn of mind.

—Nancy Allison McKinley, describing her son William

William McKinley Jr. was born on January 29, 1843, in the tiny town of Niles, Ohio. Located in the northeastern corner of Ohio, Niles had tree-shaded unpaved streets, a country store, a small church, and a bridge across Mosquito Creek. McKinley's childhood home was a long, two-storied frame house with many windows. The village grocery store took up the lower floor, and the McKinley family lived on the second floor. William was the seventh of nine children born to William McKinley Sr. and Nancy Allison McKinley.

WILLIAM MCKINLEY SR. AND MOTHER MCKINLEY

William's father, William McKinley Sr., came from a long line of hardy Scotch-Irishmen. One of fourteen children,

William and his family lived on the top floor
of this building in Niles, Ohio.

McKinley Sr. began earning his own living at the age of sixteen. A physically strong man, he knew many trades. He
forged iron, managed blast furnaces, built houses, and
mended fences. He also plowed fields and tended animals.

William McKinley Sr. married Nancy Allison in January
1829. Nancy Allison McKinley, known as "Mother
McKinley," was a deeply religious woman. She and her sister swept, scrubbed, and painted the Methodist church in
Niles. One church member said they "ran the church, all
but the preaching." Mother McKinley often cared for sick
friends. She opened her home to visiting ministers and
teachers. According to one of William's childhood friends,
"Mother McKinley was the leader in Niles of much that
was good."

*William's father and mother (shown here later in their lives)
valued religion and education.*

McKinley Sr. often traveled for his work, so Mother McKinley raised the children by herself. She and her son William were very close. She encouraged William to use all his talents. She also taught him the value of prayer, courtesy, and honesty.

LIFE IN OHIO

William attended a one-room schoolhouse in Niles. Boys and girls sat on opposite sides of the room. His first teacher, Alva Sanford, once sent William to the girls' side of the room and placed him between two girls as punishment for breaking a class rule. William seemed to enjoy it. He worked hard and was a good student. William Morrison, his second teacher, described him as "a genial, clean, bright boy and a general favorite." Morrison often placed William at a desk in the front of the class "in order to give other students a chance to plod through what he seemed to learn at a glance."

In addition to school, young William had chores at home. He drove the milk cows to the pasture each morning and back to the farm each evening. He liked to go barefoot, even in cold weather. He used to press his bare feet into the warm earth where the cows had lain. He called the feeling "pure luxury."

In his free time, William played marbles. He made and flew kites. He spent hours shooting his bow and arrows. He was a good shot and could hit almost anything. William and his friends liked to play in the "old swimmin' hole" in Mosquito Creek. Once he nearly drowned there.

William jumped in to the creek with his friends and began sinking. He couldn't swim. His friend, Joseph Butler, swam to him and tried to hold him up. Then Joseph started sinking too. Luckily, an older boy, Jacob Sheler, came along and rescued them.

William's father loved books. With only an elementary school education, William Sr. read books by English playwright William Shakespeare, Scottish poet Robert Burns, and novelist Sir Walter Scott. Friends noticed he read so much he wore the pages thin on his books. McKinley Sr. filled the house with newspapers and magazines. When William Sr. wasn't traveling for his work, the family gathered in the sitting room to read aloud each evening.

William's parents felt education was the key to a better life. They wanted more for their children than the school in Niles provided. In 1852, when William was nine, the family moved ten miles south to Poland, Ohio. The children attended high school at the Poland Academy. The new McKinley home was a large white frame house surrounded by maple trees and a white picket fence.

STUDIOUS AND DEVOUT

At the Poland Academy, William enjoyed reading, debating, and public speaking. He joined the Everett Literary and Debating Society. The group discussed literature, history, philosophy, and the important issues of the day. Slavery was the subject of many debates. The nation was becoming increasingly divided over the issue. William spent hours reading, studying, and preparing for debates. "He was always studying, studying, studying all the time," said one of his friends.

Religion played an important part in William's early life. At a religious camp meeting in 1859, when he was sixteen, he stood and announced his intention to lead a Christian life. "God is the being above all to be loved, and served," he said. "Religion seems to me to be the best thing in all the world. Here I take my stand for life." Shortly afterward he was baptized in a stream near Poland. His mother hoped William would become a minister.

In the fall of 1860, William enrolled in Allegheny College in nearby Meadville, Pennsylvania. He became ill during the winter of 1860 and returned home. When he was well enough to go back to school, his parents could not afford to send him.

William got a job to earn the money for school. He worked as a clerk in the post office in Poland. When a teaching position became available in the Kerr school district, he applied for the position and was hired.

William, at the age of sixteen, taught in the Kerr school district.

✧ ─────────────

The school was located three miles from his parents' home. Most of the time, he lived at home and walked the three miles to the school and back. At other times, he boarded with families who lived close to the school. He was a handsome young man, with thick dark hair and hazel-tinted, blue-gray eyes. His courtesy, kindness, and respect for others made him a popular teacher.

A CHANGE OF PLANS

William's teaching career was cut short by events sweeping the nation. The bitter debate over slavery, combined with other issues, led eleven Southern states to secede, or break away, from the United States. They formed the Confederate States of America. On April 12, 1861, the Civil War

(1861–1865) began with the Confederate attack on Fort Sumter, South Carolina.

The Northern states, including Ohio, prepared for war. President Abraham Lincoln called for volunteers to fight in the Union (Northern) army. In Poland, Ohio, patriotism and loyalty to the Union were strongly held beliefs. William thought the Union should be preserved, whatever the cost. He also felt slavery should be abolished.

The citizens of Poland held a meeting to discuss the war. William and his cousin, Will Osborne, listened to the speeches. After thinking the matter over carefully, they decided to enlist in the Union army. The two young men headed for Camp Jackson near Cleveland, Ohio. When they arrived at camp, Captain John C. Robinson asked William how old he was and if he had his parents' permission to enlist. At five feet six and one-quarter inches tall and weighing 125 pounds, William looked younger than his eighteen years.

William told Captain Robinson that he was old enough to enlist and that

———————— ✧

William enlisted in the Union army at the age of eighteen.

he had his parents' consent. On June 13, 1861, he and his cousin Will were mustered (enrolled) into the 23rd regiment of the Ohio Volunteer Infantry as privates. Their enlistment was for three years.

In a letter to his sister Anna, William explained his reason for joining the army. "I volunteered to serve my country in this her perilous hour from a sense of duty. I felt it was obligatory upon me, as a young man a citizen of this highly favored land, to step forward at the call of my country, and assist if possible in suppressing rebellion and putting down secession." William agreed with President Lincoln that the United States should not be split into two separate countries. He wanted to do his part to hold the United States together as one nation. Yet he knew nothing of war and had no idea of the sacrifices that were to come.

McKinley reported to Camp Jackson, Ohio, to start his military career.

CHAPTER TWO

FROM PRIVATE TO BREVET MAJOR

Every one admires him as one of the bravest and finest young officers in the army.

—Brigadier general and future president Rutherford B. Hayes, describing William McKinley in a letter

At Camp Jackson, William McKinley and the other new soldiers learned military drills. They shared guard duty and studied military tactics. In his spare time, McKinley read a book of poems by the great English poet Lord Byron. He began a diary and wrote letters for the *Mahoning Register*, a newspaper in Youngstown, Ohio. In one letter to the *Register*, he wrote, "Our boys are all determined to stand by the stars and stripes, and never give up until their lives are sacrificed, or the Government placed on a firm and solid foundation."

McKinley's regiment became known as the "psalm-singers of the Western Reserve" because of the many prayer meetings they held in camp. McKinley often attended these meetings. After one meeting, he wrote in his diary, "All day I felt the love of God in my heart and notwithstanding the surroundings there was an inward calmness and tranquility which belongs to the Christian alone."

On September 10, 1861, McKinley's regiment met the enemy for the first time at the Battle of Carnifex Ferry in western Virginia. According to McKinley's diary, "At twenty-four minutes past three, the firing commenced, and for over three hours the booming of the cannon, the report of muskets could be distinctly heard, and the smoke could be seen rising to the Heavens. . . . Frequently the cannon balls whizzed past our heads." The fighting ended as darkness fell. The Confederate forces retreated.

"This was our first real fight," said McKinley, "and the effect of the victory was of far more consequence to us than the battle itself. It gave us confidence in ourselves and faith in our commander. We learned that we could fight and whip the rebels on their own ground."

In April 1862, McKinley was promoted to commissary (supply) sergeant. His job was to make sure his regiment had plenty of food. He rode to the commissary store behind the front lines every few days with a group of soldiers and selected enough food for approximately one thousand men. Each item had to be weighed and accounted for. McKinley and his soldiers loaded the food onto mule-drawn wagons or on the backs of mules and carried it back to camp. Then they unloaded it and issued it to the cooks. McKinley also made sure the horses and mules were fed.

Commissary Sergeant McKinley took his job seriously. If he couldn't find enough food at the commissary store, he found what he could in the surrounding countryside.

Rutherford B. Hayes

——————— ✧ ———————

According to Rutherford B. Hayes, "Young as he was, we soon found that in business, in executive ability, young McKinley was a man of rare capacity, of unusual and unsurpassed capacity, especially for a boy of his age."

A SOLDIER AND A GENTLEMAN

McKinley's regiment marched to Princeton, West Virginia, in late April. They found the town in flames. Confederate troops had set fire to the town in order to destroy supplies and prevent Union forces from getting them. When the Union troops arrived, they began looting. As McKinley rode past the home of a wealthy family, a woman who lived in the house stopped him. She was furious that Union soldiers were taking things from her home. She asked McKinley whether or not there were any gentlemen in the Yankee army.

McKinley tipped his hat and replied, "Madam, I pass for one at my home in Ohio, and I shall see at once that these annoyances cease." He placed a guard in front of the house, and the looting stopped.

A DARING DELIVERY

On September 17, 1862, McKinley took part in the bloodiest single-day battle in U.S. history. The Battle of

Antietam, in western Maryland, began early in the morning. The men had gone into battle without breakfast. By late afternoon, they were tired, hungry, and thirsty. As commissary sergeant, it was McKinley's duty to feed the troops. He rounded up some soldiers and rode back to the store, about two miles behind the battlefield. He ordered the men to load an army wagon with cooked meat, pork and beans, crackers, and hot coffee. Then he hitched two mules to the wagon and made a mad dash to the front line of battle.

The weary soldiers noticed an army wagon headed toward them "at breakneck speed, through a terrific fire of musketry and artillery that seemed to threaten annihilation to everything within its range." The men cheered when they realized the wagon carried food. Keeping a cool head, McKinley fed the troops. According to Rutherford B. Hayes, "From his hands every man in the regiment was served with hot coffee and warm meats, a thing that had never occurred under similar circumstances in any other army in the world."

A FINE YOUNG OFFICER

McKinley's bravery at Antietam earned him a promotion. He became an officer with the rank of second lieutenant. In January 1863, Colonel Hayes made him the brigade quartermaster. McKinley's new job meant more responsibility. He was in charge of ordering all supplies for his brigade. Everything a soldier needed came from the quartermaster—clothing, equipment, tents, stoves, flags, musical instruments, tools, wagons, horses, and mules. McKinley recorded each item and kept up with thousands of details. He filled out endless paperwork and sent copies of his reports to the quartermaster general in Washington.

The soldiers respected Lieutenant McKinley. He got along well with the enlisted men and his superior officers. Serious by nature, McKinley also showed a sense of humor at times. He once bragged that he could shave with a straight razor using his left hand or his right hand. His friends bet he could not. McKinley demonstrated his unique talent by shaving the left side of his face with his left hand and the right side of his face with his right hand. He won the bet without a single nick on his smooth chin.

McKinley rose quickly through the army ranks. In March 1863, he was promoted to first lieutenant. At the Battle of Kernstown in Virginia on July 24, 1864, one Union regiment was trapped in an orchard while the rest of the Union forces retreated. As the Confederate troops advanced, Colonel Hayes ordered McKinley to ride out to the nearly surrounded regiment and lead them to safety. McKinley mounted his little brown horse and galloped into the thick of the battle. "None of us expected to see him again, as we watched him push his horse through the open fields, over fences, through ditches, while a well-directed fire from the enemy was poured upon him, with shells exploding around, about and over him," said one witness. "Once he was completely enveloped in the smoke of an exploding shell, and we thought he had gone down."

The smoke cleared to show McKinley, still seated on his bob-tailed horse, had reached the regiment. He ordered them to retreat and led the men to safety. The day after the battle, McKinley was promoted again, this time to captain.

Shortly after his promotion, General George Crook asked to have McKinley placed on his staff. During the Battle of Opequan in Virginia, McKinley carried verbal orders to

General Isaac Duval to move his division to a new position. The orders didn't specify which route Duval's men should take, so McKinley suggested they take a route by the creek.

Duval told McKinley he would not budge without definite orders from General Crook. McKinley straightened himself in the saddle, saluted, and said, "This is a case of great emergency, general. I order you, by command of General Crook." It was a risky move on McKinley's part. If the order had led to disaster, he would have faced serious consequences. General Duval moved his division as McKinley directed, and the men arrived safely at their new position.

Twenty-one-year-old Captain McKinley voted in his first presidential election on November 8, 1864. A battered army ambulance served as the election booth. He voted for Abraham Lincoln.

✧ ————————

General Crook was well liked by his men. Rutherford B. Hayes even named one of his children after him.

McKinley, twenty-two, was given the honorary title of brevet major by President Abraham Lincoln.

——————————— ✧

President Lincoln appointed McKinley brevet major in March 1865 for "gallant and meritorious services." On April 9, 1865, Confederate general Robert E. Lee surrendered to Ulysses S. Grant at Appomattox Court House in Virginia. The Civil War was over.

McKinley officially ended his army career on July 26, 1865. He had entered the war a boy. He came out a mature man. Confident and self-assured, McKinley carried himself ramrod straight and walked at a brisk pace. He returned home to Poland, Ohio, anxious to begin life as a civilian but unsure which direction his life would take.

McKinley in 1866

CHAPTER THREE

OHIO LAWYER

Major Wm. McKinley is a good lawyer, a fine orator, and both in respect to ability and character, commands the respect and esteem of his fellow citizens.

—Canton Repository and Republican, October 7, 1869

When twenty-two-year-old William McKinley arrived home after the war, he needed to find a job. He was ambitious, but his goal was not great wealth. He wanted a position of importance and high status in the community. He also felt intense patriotism and longed to serve his country in peace as he had in war. Major McKinley, using a title that stayed with him after the war, considered many different careers.

He thought of returning to the army as a professional soldier, but his father argued against it. His mother urged him to become a minister, but he did not feel called to the ministry. His friend and former commander, Rutherford B. Hayes, advised him to move west and become a businessman.

A STUDENT OF THE LAW

McKinley considered his options and decided to become a lawyer. He studied in the law office of Judge Charles Glidden, the area's best-known attorney. Thirty-year-old Glidden had a superb grasp of the law and an eloquent speaking voice. McKinley arrived at his office early every morning and read law books until late at night. He watched Glidden and learned as much as he could about the law.

In September 1866, Glidden encouraged McKinley to attend law school. With financial help from his sister Anna, McKinley enrolled in Albany Law School in Albany, New York. He studied hard but also loved the social life. He often attended the theater. He went to parties, teas, and receptions. He was popular with the girls and well liked among his fellow classmates. According to his roommate, George F. Arrel, McKinley "was a delightful companion. He was jolly, always good-natured, and looked at the bright side of everything."

As much as he enjoyed a good time, McKinley did not let his social life interfere with his studies. "He worked very hard, often reading until one or two o'clock in the morning," recalled his roommate. "It was his very great industry, rather than genius, that paved the way for his success."

In the spring of 1867, McKinley passed the bar exam (a test lawyers must take to prove their qualifications) and was admitted to the Ohio Bar Association. The young lawyer moved to Canton, Ohio, where his sister Anna worked as the principal of the grammar school. Located in the heart of a rich farming district, Canton was a thriving city. It boasted an open square in the center of town and streets laid out like a checkerboard. With family nearby, McKinley found Canton an ideal place to begin his law practice.

CANTON'S YOUNG LAWYER

McKinley rented a small office in a bank building. Attorney George W. Belden worked in the same building. Belden was impressed with the young lawyer. He strolled into McKinley's office one evening and dropped a pile of papers on his desk. Belden explained that he didn't feel well but had to appear in court the next morning to try a case. He asked McKinley to take over the case for him. McKinley tried to refuse. He told Belden that he didn't have enough time to prepare. Belden convinced McKinley by telling him if he didn't try the case, it wouldn't be heard.

McKinley spent the night poring over the pile of trial documents. The next morning, he appeared in court for the first time. As he stood to begin his argument, he glanced back and saw Belden seated at the back of the courtroom, a slight smile on his lips. Belden had tricked him! McKinley argued the case and won.

Several days later, Belden visited McKinley and dropped twenty-five dollars on his desk. McKinley protested. Twenty-five dollars was too much money for one day of work. Belden laughed, pressed the money into his hand and said, "It's all right, Mac, I got a hundred." The two became partners, and McKinley built up a successful law practice in Canton.

CAMPAIGNING FOR FRIENDS

In the fall of 1867, McKinley entered the world of politics. He campaigned for his old friend, Rutherford B. Hayes, who was running for governor of Ohio. McKinley spoke for Hayes from the top of a wooden crate in North Canton. He then repeated the speech around Stark County. McKinley

A campaign banner shows the slogan of Ulysses S. Grant in his bid for the presidency.

———————————— ◇

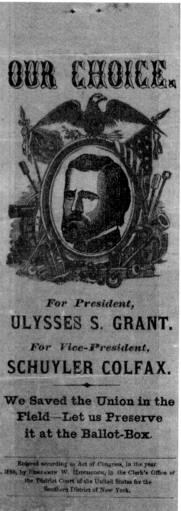

OUR CHOICE.

For President,
ULYSSES S. GRANT.
For Vice-President,
SCHUYLER COLFAX.

We Saved the Union in the Field—Let us Preserve it at the Ballot-Box.

Entered according to Act of Congress, in the year 1868, by Benjamin W. Hitchcock, in the Clerk's Office of the District Court of the United States for the Southern District of New York.

also gave speeches in support of voting rights for newly freed male slaves. He believed that since African Americans had fought in the war, they should be awarded every constitutional right in peace.

A year later, McKinley became chairman of the Republican Central Committee for Stark County. He supported Republican presidential candidate Ulysses S. Grant. McKinley organized Grant for President clubs and gave speeches supporting Grant. The young lawyer's strong speaking skills proved an asset to the Republican Party. Both Hayes and Grant won their elections.

In 1869 McKinley ran for his first elected office—prosecuting attorney of Stark County. Republican McKinley was not expected to win in Democratic Stark County. He campaigned vigorously and, to everyone's surprise, won the election. Things were going well for McKinley, both professionally and personally. He was serving his country through an elected office and had found the woman of his dreams, Ida Saxton.

Ida Saxton
——————— ✧ ———————

IDA

Ida was a beautiful young woman, with sky blue eyes, fair skin, and auburn hair. The daughter of a prominent banker and businessman, she attended the Brook Hall Seminary in Medea, Pennsylvania. Like other wealthy, educated young women in 1869, Ida spent seven months touring the capitals of Europe with her sister and a group of friends. Bright, witty, and vivacious, Ida was generous and warm-hearted. She was also sensitive, nervous, and high-strung.

In the late-1800s, most wealthy women did not work outside the home. Ida's father did not agree with the limited options available for women. He believed his daughters should be able to support themselves and earn a living if necessary. When Ida returned from her tour of Europe, she worked as a cashier in her father's bank. She soon attracted the attention of many of Canton's eligible young bachelors. William McKinley was one of them. He increased his visits to the bank and often took Ida out riding in his carriage. McKinley fell deeply in love with Ida. She adored him.

McKinley married Ida Saxton in this church in Canton, Ohio.

✧ —————————

William and Ida were married on January 25, 1871, in the First Presbyterian Church of Canton. Ida wore an ivory satin and lace gown. The newlyweds traveled to New York City for their honeymoon. For a wedding gift, Ida's father gave them a white frame house on North Market Street in Canton, telling McKinley, "You are the only man I have ever known to whom I would entrust my daughter."

In the summer of 1871, McKinley ran for a second term as prosecuting attorney. He lost the election, but the happiness of his family life softened the disappointment of the election results. He was about to become a father.

CHILDREN AND TRAGEDY

Ida gave birth to Katherine, the McKinley's first child, on Christmas Day, 1871. Called Katie by her doting parents, William and Ida adored their beautiful child. She became the center of their universe. Two years later, the couple prepared for the addition of a second child to their family.

Ida's mother died in the spring of 1873, just before the birth of their second child. Ida was grief-stricken. She and her mother had been extremely close. After a long and difficult labor, Ida gave birth to baby Ida on April 1, 1873. The baby was frail and sickly from birth. She died four months later.

Ida became depressed and spent days in bed. Obsessed with protecting Katie, Ida sat for hours in a darkened room, holding her daughter on her lap and weeping. Her overwhelming grief affected the young girl. Uncle Abner McKinley once found Katie swinging on a garden gate and invited her to go for a walk with him. Katie replied, "No, I mustn't go out of the yard or God'll punish mamma some more."

In June 1875, the family suffered another tragedy. Katie died of typhoid fever. McKinley was devastated. Ida became severely depressed, a semi-invalid who needed constant care. She suffered from phlebitis, which crippled her legs and made walking painful. She also developed epilepsy, a disease for which no treatment existed in the nineteenth century. The disease caused frequent headaches, fainting spells, and, sometimes, violent seizures. Doctors could do little for Ida, so they used a variety of narcotics to calm her. As Ida's

McKinley's daughters, Katie and Ida, are buried next to each other in Canton, Ohio.

✧ ————————————

physical health faded, she grew extremely possessive of her husband and was anxious whenever he was away from her. McKinley patiently nursed Ida through one illness after another. He became known for his devotion to her.

The heartache of his personal life altered McKinley. According to biographer Thomas Beer, "His buoyant manner changed. He became a soft-spoken, watchful nurse in his own house and a worried guest if he was in company without his charge." To cope with his grief and worries, he threw himself into his work.

ON THE CAMPAIGN TRAIL

In 1876 McKinley campaigned for presidential candidate Rutherford B. Hayes. He also campaigned for himself. McKinley had decided to run for a seat in the U.S. Congress. He went on rounds with a local doctor and shook hands with patients. He smiled at babies and chatted with people of all ages. He visited remote villages and country farms. He spoke at sawmills and barbershops.

McKinley was known for his dynamic speeches. He spoke with a musical voice, and his simple persuasiveness carried conviction. He had a knack for winning voters to his views. They came to believe in him and trust him.

When the election results came in, McKinley and his friend Hayes both celebrated victories. McKinley prepared to represent Ohio's Eighteenth District in the House of Representatives. He and Ida packed their bags, said their good-byes, and headed for Washington.

The McKinleys lived in the Ebbitt House Hotel in Washington, D.C.,
throughout McKinley's time in the U.S. House of Representatives.

CHAPTER FOUR

CONGRESSMAN McKINLEY

My opponents in Congress go at me tooth and nail, but they always apologize to William when they are going to call him names.

—Thomas Reed, congressman from Maine

Early in 1877, thirty-three-year-old Congressman McKinley and his wife, Ida, moved into the Ebbitt House Hotel in Washington, D.C. They lived in a small suite of two rooms. One room served as McKinley's workroom, the other as a bedroom.

McKinley's days followed a fixed routine. He rose early, picked up his mail and newspapers, and worked for a couple of hours before he ate breakfast with Ida. He usually walked to his office or the House of Representatives, wearing a dark double-breasted frock coat. A red carnation, his favorite flower, could always be found in his lapel.

McKinley had an advantage over most freshmen congressmen. He often visited his friend and mentor President

Hayes at the White House. This privilege would not have been available to him if another man had occupied the Oval Office.

A TIRELESS WORKER

Congressman McKinley worked hard and always tried to satisfy the various needs of his constituents. He carefully studied each proposed law and earned a reputation as "industrious, well-informed, and level-headed." In discussions on the House floor, McKinley spoke with force and conviction. He knew how to present complicated subjects in simple, understandable language. He had an excellent memory for figures and could back up his position with columns of statistics. McKinley supported civil service laws to employ only qualified people in government jobs. He favored antiliquor laws and women's suffrage, or voting rights for women. He spoke out against injustices against African Americans in the South.

McKinley's specialty became the protective tariff, a tax on imported goods. Many U.S. industries lost money because foreign companies could make products cheaper than U.S. companies. The U.S. economy suffered when imported foreign products sold for lower prices than U.S.-made products. The protective tariff taxed these imported goods. It encouraged Americans to buy U.S.-made goods. It also provided funds to operate the government.

McKinley became an expert on the subject. He believed a high protective tariff would solve the country's economic woes. He studied the history of protection and tariff laws. He read the views of experts on the subject, such as Alexander Hamilton and Henry Clay. He spent hours listening to people argue for and against protective tariffs. He visited thousands of workers and toured factories, farms, and mines.

"I believe that it is the duty of American Congressmen to legislate for American citizens, and not for foreign manufacturers," he said in one speech. "Let us take care of our own interests, and look to the well-being of our own citizens first." McKinley's stand on the tariff made him popular with voters.

CONSTANT CAMPAIGNING

Congressmen serve two-year terms, and McKinley, a Republican, fought a fierce battle for reelection in 1878. The Democratic Party was then the majority party in Ohio. To give the Democratic candidate a better chance of winning the election, the Ohio legislature changed Ohio's district boundaries. The new boundaries concentrated Democratic neighborhoods in McKinley's district. The newly drawn district gave the Democratic candidate an advantage. This process is known as gerrymandering. "The redistricting was not in the interest of fairness, but to increase Democratic representation, in violation of every principle of fairness," said McKinley. He worked day and night, traveled throughout the district, and gave hundreds of speeches. He won in spite of the redistricting.

In 1880 McKinley won a third reelection and was appointed to the House Ways and Means Committee. This important committee was responsible for raising money to finance the U.S. government. The committee made recommendations on tariff legislation. As an expert on tariffs, McKinley became a vital part of the committee.

RANDOM ACTS OF KINDNESS

William McKinley was known for his countless acts of kindness. He often took the red carnation from his lapel and gave it to a visitor. He genuinely liked people and always tried to do what he could for them. His colleague Elihu Root said of him, "He was more thoughtful of others than any other man I ever knew."

During one of McKinley's congressional campaigns, a reporter for his opponent followed him wherever he went and printed unfavorable stories about McKinley. McKinley had noticed the man because he looked unwell and had a persistent cough. One cold and blustery night, McKinley rode in a closed carriage to a neighboring town to give a speech. He heard the familiar cough of his adversary coming from the open seat of the driver. McKinley stopped the carriage and ordered the reporter to get down.

The reporter expected to be sent away. Instead, McKinley gave the man his overcoat and invited him into the carriage. "But, Major McKinley," replied the astonished reporter, "I guess you don't know who I am. I have been with you the whole campaign, giving it to you every time you spoke and I am going over to-night to rip you to pieces if I can."

"I know," said McKinley, "but you put on this coat and get inside so you can do a better job."

McKinley's 1882 reelection campaign pitted him against Democratic candidate Jonathan Wallace. McKinley won by eight votes, but Wallace claimed to have received more votes and contested the election. A congressional committee investigated and found that some of the ballots did not contain Wallace's full name. When the "J. Wallace" and "John Wallace" votes were added to Wallace's total, Wallace clearly won the election. In May 1884, more than eighteen months after the election, the Committee on Elections voted to give McKinley's seat in the House of Representatives to Wallace. McKinley returned to Ohio to campaign for Republican presidential candidate James G. Blaine.

One month later, McKinley attended the Republican National Convention in Chicago, Illinois. He presented the Republican platform, or the aims and principles of the Republican Party. McKinley gained national attention for his commanding presence. Determined to win back his seat in the House of Representatives, McKinley campaigned hard throughout the summer and fall. In October 1884, he won his reelection campaign and returned to Congress.

TAKING CARE OF IDA

Ida's delicate health did not allow the McKinleys to take part in Washington's social whirl. The couple spent most of their evenings alone or with a small group of friends. They entertained guests in McKinley's workroom or downstairs in the parlor.

Caring for Ida was McKinley's chief concern. He hired a personal maid for her. When he left Washington, he wrote to her at least once a day. When he worked late, he sent a note to the Ebbitt House Hotel, telling her when to expect

House of Representatives U.S.,

Washington, D.C., *April 10*, 1888.

My darling wife:

It looks now as though I would not get home tonight, the opposition seem determined to eek it out and nothing remains for us but to stay with them, which we will do, unless later on we can take a recess. I congratulate myself that I am feeling splendidly and am fully able for the night. I hope you will get a good nights sleep; Receive my evening benediction of love. If I don't see you tonight, will be with you some time in the morning. Goodnight and may the good angels guard you.

Lovingly,
Wm McKinley Jr

McKinley's devotion to his wife was shown through notes, such as this one, letting her know he might not be home that night.
✧ ——————

him. People throughout the country admired McKinley for his devotion to his wife.

DEVELOPING DIPLOMACY

McKinley's patience with his wife carried over to his work in Congress. He was known as the only man in Congress who had no enemies. "He had a rare tact as a manager of men," said Wisconsin congressman Robert La Follette. "Back of his courteous and affable manner was a firmness that never yielded conviction, and while scarcely seeming to force issues he usually achieved exactly what he sought."

Others noted his honesty, thoroughness, and ability to bring together people with conflicting views. He had a knack for smoothing hurt feelings and persuading opponents to compromise. According to La Follette, McKinley often said, "Come now, let us put the personal element aside and consider the principle involved."

Robert La Follette

A NATIONAL FIGURE

In June 1888, McKinley attended the Republican National Convention in Chicago. Once again, he read the Republican platform before the convention. During the convention, a group of delegates tried to nominate him for president. But McKinley had already promised to support someone else, U.S. Senator John Sherman.

To stop the flood of support heading his way, McKinley leaped onto a chair and announced in no uncertain terms that he was not a candidate for president. "I can not," he said, "consistently with my own views of personal integrity, consent, or seem to consent, to permit my name to be used as a candidate before this Convention. I would not respect myself if I could find it in my heart to do so."

The Republicans chose U.S. senator Benjamin Harrison instead of Sherman. McKinley earned high praise for refusing to be nominated and sticking by his man. He emerged from the convention with his reputation brighter than ever.

THE MCKINLEY TARIFF

The Republican Party nominated McKinley for Speaker of the House of Representatives in 1889. He lost to Thomas B. Reed of Maine. Reed appointed McKinley chairman of the House Ways and Means Committee.

In his first act as chairman, McKinley announced he would hold hearings on a new tariff bill. Day after day, he sat and listened to a parade of witnesses. He smoked one cigar after another, took notes, and eventually produced 1,400 pages of testimony. On May 7, 1890, he summarized the committee's findings and introduced a new tariff bill in the House of Representatives.

His plan rested on two points: the tariff produced higher wages for U.S. workers, and U.S. businesses were not developed enough to face foreign competition. "With me this position is a deep conviction, not a theory," he said. "I believe in it and thus warmly advocate it because enveloped in it are my country's highest development and greatest prosperity; out of it come the greatest gains to the people, the greatest comforts to the masses. . . ."

A lengthy debate took place in the House and Senate where 450 amendments were added to the bill. Finally, on October 1, 1890, President Harrison signed the McKinley

Tariff into law. It taxed nearly four thousand imported items. U.S. businesses liked the McKinley Tariff, but most consumers did not. They feared prices would go up. Democrats reinforced this fear and attacked the bill during the congressional campaigns of 1890.

The Ohio legislature gerrymandered Ohio's district boundaries again, giving McKinley's district a large Democratic margin. After thirteen years in Congress, McKinley lost the 1890 election. He and Ida returned home to Ohio with no definite plans for the future.

McKinley became governor of Ohio in 1892.

CHAPTER FIVE

GOVERNOR McKINLEY

*The best government always is that
one which best looks after its own and
which is in closest heart touch with the
highest aspirations of the people.*

—William McKinley, second inaugural address as
governor of Ohio, January 8, 1894

Republican leaders in Ohio began plans to nominate
McKinley for governor in 1891. McKinley hesitated. He
had just lost his congressional seat and was not eager to
face defeat again in his home state.

At the Ohio Republican Convention in June, crowds
cheered when McKinley appeared. He agreed to run for governor. "I accept the nomination you have tendered me, sen-
sible both of the honor and responsibility it implies," he said.
"It is a summons of my party to duty which I can not disre-
gard and to which I yield cheerful obedience." He won the
election against Democratic incumbent James E. Campbell.

The McKinleys lived in the Neil House (above)
for most of his time as governor.

SETTLING IN AS GOVERNOR

The McKinleys moved into a suite of rooms at the Chittenden Hotel in Columbus, Ohio, across from the Ohio Statehouse. When the Chittenden burned down, they moved to a new suite in the nearby Neil House. Their Neil House apartment consisted of an office, parlor, bedroom, dining room, storeroom, and maid's quarters.

McKinley walked across the street to his office each morning, carrying several newspapers and a fresh supply of cigars. He loved smoking cigars but carefully avoided being photographed with one because it set a bad example for children. Reportedly, he smoked twenty cigars a day.

Before he entered the Statehouse, McKinley turned and waved to Ida. At precisely 3:00 each afternoon, regardless of what he was doing, he would open his window and wave a white handkerchief to his wife. She sat at the window of their hotel waiting for this sign of affection from her "dearest."

Despite her poor health, Ida attended formal state dinners with her husband. He always sat next to her at dinner so that he could drop a handkerchief over her face if she had an epileptic seizure. When the seizure passed, McKinley removed the handkerchief and resumed the conversation as if nothing had happened.

The new governor began his term by recommending safety devices for railroad employees and other workers in dangerous jobs. He steered a law through the Ohio legislature to prevent and settle conflicts between workers and their employers. McKinley also created a commission of experts to study Ohio's tax system. He developed a tax system that placed taxes on corporations and reduced Ohio's debt.

ECONOMIC DISASTER

In 1893 an economic depression hit the United States. Banks closed, businesses went bankrupt, and many people lost their jobs. The depression affected McKinley in February 1893 and nearly cost him his political career.

Robert L. Walker, a Poland, Ohio, banker and manufacturer, had been McKinley's friend since childhood. When Walker needed money for his business, McKinley endorsed, or promised to pay, Walker's loans. Walker's business collapsed in 1893, and McKinley was held responsible for a debt of $130,000—about $2.5 million in modern money.

Haggard and drawn, with dark circles under his eyes, McKinley paced the floors at night, unable to sleep. He thought about leaving politics and returning to the practice of law so he could pay the debt. He feared his political career was over.

Businessman Mark Hanna and a group of McKinley's friends set up a trust fund to raise money to pay the debt. McKinley assigned his property to the trust. Ida contributed her inheritance. When friends tried to discourage her from donating the money her father had left her, Ida snapped, "My husband has done everything for me all my life. Do you mean to deny me the privilege of doing as I please with my own property to help him now?" A group of wealthy friends, including John Hay, Andrew Carnegie, and Philander C. Knox, contributed to the fund. By September the debt was paid, and the McKinleys' property was returned to them.

McKinley's financial woes didn't hurt him in the polls. He was reelected governor in 1893 by a large majority. (At this time, a governor served a two-year term.) Rather than hurt his political career, McKinley's money problems enhanced his reputation as one of the people. They sympathized with him and respected his lack of interest in accumulating wealth.

A FIRM HAND

The economic depression affected people throughout Ohio and the entire nation. Violent labor strikes accompanied the high unemployment rates. McKinley identified with the working class, but he would not tolerate violence. In the spring of 1894, striking coal miners seized trains, tore up railroad tracks, and threw rocks at railroad crews. McKinley called out the Ohio National Guard.

"I do not care if my political career is not twenty-four hours long," he told one group of strikers, "these outrages must stop if it takes every soldier in Ohio." Time and again, McKinley sent troops to restore order during the dark days of the depression. Because of his winning personality, he was able to do so without destroying his reputation with Ohio's labor force.

In 1895 McKinley announced he would not seek a third term as governor of Ohio. He campaigned for Republican candidate Asa Bushnell. When Bushnell won the election, the McKinleys left the state capital and returned to their old home on North Market Street in Canton, Ohio.

A NEW GOAL

McKinley decided the time was right to run for president of the United States. The country blamed Democratic president Grover Cleveland for the economic hard times. Politically savvy McKinley sensed the country's desire for change. The next election would be won by a Republican, and as a prominent leader in the Republican Party, McKinley saw 1896 as his year.

Mark Hanna, his campaign manager, rented a house in Thomasville, Georgia, and invited the McKinleys for a visit. Hanna also invited important political bosses from the South. Although McKinley called the vacation "a little rest and outing," it was more a political move than a vacation. Many influential Republicans from the South got a chance to meet the candidate and hear what he had to say.

Political bosses in Pennsylvania and New York offered to support McKinley's bid for the presidency if McKinley gave them jobs in the new administration. They wanted to be cabinet members (people who advise the president on important issues). McKinley refused. He thought cabinet positions should be given to the people most qualified for the jobs, not as political favors. "Some things come too high," he told Mark Hanna. "If I were to accept the nomination on those terms, the place would be worth nothing to me and less to the people. If those are the terms, I am out of it."

By the summer of 1896, as Republicans prepared for their national convention, McKinley was the heavy favorite. "He may die before the convention meets or be incapacitated by paralysis, but hardly any other event can deprive him of his present advantage," reported the *Brooklyn Daily Eagle*. When Senator Joseph B. Foraker of Ohio placed McKinley's name before the convention as a candidate for president, the cheering went on for twenty-seven minutes. In July the Democrats chose William Jennings Bryan to oppose McKinley.

William Jennings Bryan speaks to a crowd from a railroad train during his 1896 campaign for the presidency.

AN EXCITING CAMPAIGN

Handsome, thirty-six-year-old Bryan rode his private train across the United States on a whirlwind campaign tour. He was full of charisma. His speeches were vibrant and dramatic. McKinley knew he couldn't compete with Bryan as a speaker. "I might just as well put up a trapeze on my front lawn and compete with some professional athlete as go out speaking against Bryan," he said. "I have to *think* when I speak." McKinley chose to stay home and let the people come to him. Railroads offered discounted fares to Canton, and delegations from around the country poured onto his front lawn.

McKinley made himself available to anyone who cared to visit, at all hours, every day but Sunday. He welcomed the crowds to his home, gave carefully prepared speeches, and handed out pamphlets stating his views. McKinley tailored his speeches for each audience. He was known for his plain, common-sense language, his wide knowledge on a variety of subjects, and his sincerity. He spoke softly at first, then gradually increased the strength of his voice until he thundered at the end like an inspirational preacher.

After each speech, he held informal receptions on his front porch and shook hands with visitors. McKinley smiled at each guest. He would grasp the caller's right hand in his and squeeze it warmly, hold the man's elbow with his left hand, and then swiftly pull him along to make ready for the next person. This unique method of shaking hands became known as the McKinley grip. It was so efficient he could shake fifty hands a minute. By early October, between twenty and thirty thousand visitors descended on Canton each day. By Election Day, McKinley had spoken to more than 750,000 people from his front porch.

Battle of the Standards

U.S. currency became the central issue of the 1896 presidential campaign. McKinley and the Republicans wanted U.S. currency to be based on gold. Since gold was rare, this meant less money would be in circulation, making it more valuable. Bryan and the Democrats wanted the free and unlimited coinage of silver. This would allow more money to be printed, but it would not be worth as much. Both sides feared economic disaster if the other side won.

McKinley approached this volatile issue with caution. If he spoke too strongly in favor of gold, he would lose support in the western United States, the land of silver mines. If he favored silver, he would lose bankers and businesspeople in the eastern United States.

He focused his campaign on the idea that the gold standard would return the United States to prosperity after the depression. He adopted the campaign slogan "McKinley and the Full Dinner Pail," and he became known as the "Advance Agent of Prosperity." He assured voters that if they elected him, jobs would be available for anyone who wished to work.

Bryan, on the other hand, based his entire campaign on the money question. He focused so exclusively on promoting free silver that as the election neared, people came to believe that he had no ideas on any other issue. "His oratory was magnificent," recalled McKinley campaign worker Charles G. Dawes, "his logic pitifully weak." As Bryan's speeches became more and more radical, people feared the nation would fall apart if he were elected.

One of Bryan's supporters, L. Frank Baum, wrote the children's book *The Wonderful Wizard of Oz*. He filled the book with metaphors about the money question. In the original book, Dorothy wore silver slippers and traveled down

L. Frank Baum used many metaphors in his book The Wonderful Wizard of Oz *to promote free silver.*

✦ —————————

a sidewalk of gold to a city the color of money. To return home, Dorothy only needed to click her silver shoes together. Dorothy's solution mirrored the U.S. economic solution as outlined by William Jennings Bryan: silver would take the United States anywhere it wanted to go. When voters went to the polls, however, they chose the road paved with gold by electing William McKinley the twenty-fifth president of the United States.

McKinley shakes hands with a voter on the steps of his Canton, Ohio, home.
✧ ──────────────

Ida McKinley rarely appeared during the campaign. As a result, rumors spread that she was a lunatic, a freak, or a spy. The Republican Party printed a campaign biography about Ida to squelch the wild rumors. It was the first time a political party printed material to educate the public on a candidate's wife.

Mark Hanna raised more than $3.5 million ($71 million in modern money) for McKinley's presidential campaign. This was a record amount of money at that time. McKinley directed his campaign managers in key areas of the country by telephone. He was the first politician to use long-distance telephones during a presidential campaign. A simple motion picture of the candidate was shown in a few major cities. Paid speakers toured the country, and McKinley's speeches were printed in newspapers and pamphlets. McKinley for President clubs formed around the nation, and the candidate's face appeared on badges and buttons. According to Theodore Roosevelt, Hanna "advertised McKinley as if he were a patent medicine."

On Election Day, McKinley sat smoking one cigar after another as the election results came in. He took an early lead. By midnight he knew that at age fifty-three he had been elected president of the United States. His nephew, James McKinley, found McKinley and his wife in Mother McKinley's bedroom. "The old lady is kneeling beside the bed with one arm around the governor and the other around Aunt Ida," he recalled. "Oh, God, keep him humble," she prayed.

CHAPTER SIX

PRESIDENT McKINLEY

*We want no wars of conquest; we must avoid
the temptation of territorial aggression.
War should never be entered upon until
every agency of peace has failed.*

—William McKinley, first inaugural address,
March 4, 1897

President-elect McKinley spent the four months after his election organizing his cabinet. On March 1, 1897, he gave one last speech from Canton before leaving for his inauguration in Washington. "To all of us the future is as a sealed book," he said, "but if I can, by official act or administration or utterance, in any degree add to the prosperity and unity of our beloved country and the advancement and well-being of our splendid citizenship, I will devote the best and most unselfish efforts of my life to that end."

Inauguration Day, March 4, 1897, dawned bright and beautiful. The newspapers called it McKinley weather. The

streets were lined with cheering crowds. They waved at out-
going president Grover Cleveland and President-elect
McKinley. The two men rode together from the White
House to the U.S. Capitol Building in President Cleveland's
carriage. Fifty thousand people gathered in the plaza in
front of the Capitol to hear the oath of office administered.
For the first time in history, Thomas Edison's kinetoscope,
a motion picture camera, captured the event on film.

  President McKinley and the First Lady settled into the
White House. The ninety-seven-year-old building was
cramped and crumbling. They filled their new home with
fresh flowers and potted palms from the conservatories on
the White House grounds. The couple often played card
games with friends in the evenings. When Ida felt well
enough, they attended the theater.

———————————— ◇ ————————————

*Chief Justice Melville Weston Fuller administers the oath of office to
McKinley. President Grover Cleveland stands on the right.*

President McKinley (left) *meets with his cabinet.*

THE MCKINLEY ADMINISTRATION

President McKinley met with his cabinet on Tuesday and Friday mornings. Discussions were informal. After hearing various opinions on a problem facing the nation, McKinley made his decision. "He had a way of handling men," said cabinet member Elihu Root, "so that they thought his ideas were their own. . . . He cared nothing about the credit, but McKinley *always had his way.*"

The new president called a special session of Congress on March 15 to work out a new tariff bill. He encouraged Congress to look for ways to expand overseas markets for U.S. products. After months of debate in the Senate and House, McKinley signed the Dingley Act into law on July 24. The new law put into effect the highest protective tariff to date.

In his first year in office, McKinley pushed for the annexation, or takeover, of Hawaii. He also wanted the United States to secure the rights to dig a canal in Central America. Before these issues could be resolved, however, another problem surfaced with far more urgency in a place named Cuba.

FOREIGN AFFAIRS

When McKinley became president, he fully expected to spend his time working on domestic issues, or problems affecting the citizens of the United States. But from the beginning of his presidency, events taking place far from U.S. borders turned his attention more and more to foreign affairs.

Cuba, located ninety miles off the southern tip of Florida, was one of the last remaining overseas possessions of Spain. By 1897 Spain's global empire, which once included large parts of North, South, and Central America, had shrunk to the islands of Cuba, Puerto Rico, Guam, and the Philippines.

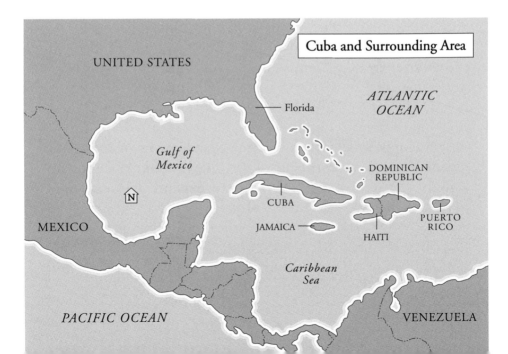

Cuba and Surrounding Area

A group of Cuban rebels was fighting a fierce battle for independence from Spain. They attacked Spanish military outposts with cries of *Cuba Libre!* (Free Cuba). They destroyed the Cuban economy by burning plantations and tearing up railroad lines. In retaliation, the Spanish military arrested many Cubans and threw them into prison camps. Unsanitary conditions and torture led to many deaths. Thousands of men, women, and children died of hunger and disease.

Many people in the United States felt that because Cuba was an immediate neighbor, the United States had a moral obligation to help. Others saw a chance for the United States to acquire its first colony and become a world power. Both groups pressured McKinley to stop the fighting in Cuba, even if it took a war.

LET'S TALK

McKinley hoped to stop the suffering in Cuba without a war. He sent William Calhoun on a fact-finding mission to Cuba. Calhoun found Cuba "wrapped in the stillness of death and the silence of desolation." McKinley appointed Stewart Woodford the U.S. minister to Spain and sent him to the Spanish capital of Madrid to negotiate a peace settlement.

In December 1897, McKinley delivered his annual message to Congress. He discussed the situation in Cuba and urged Congress and the American people to be patient with Spain. "The best sentiment of the civilized world is moving toward the settlement of differences between nations without resorting to the horrors of war," he said. He set up a Cuban relief fund to send supplies and medicines to the people of Cuba. McKinley secretly contributed $5,000 ($102,000) of his own money to the fund.

YELLOW JOURNALISM

Newspaper publishers Joseph Pulitzer, owner of the *New York World*, and William Randolph Hearst, owner of the *New York Journal*, fed the flames of U.S. public opinion against Spain. Hearst sent reporters to Cuba with instructions to send back the most outrageous stories they could find. The Spanish military, led by General Valeriano Weyler, became more and more brutal in dealing with revolutionaries. Hearst's reporters sent home graphic, shocking stories about "Butcher Weyler" and the atrocities he committed. Some of the stories were true. Others were made up or exaggerated to boost sales of Hearst's newspapers. This practice of creating the most shocking and sensational reports possible became known as yellow journalism.

In January 1898, McKinley ordered the USS *Maine,* a heavily armed battleship, to Havana, Cuba. He called the

───────────── ✧ ─────────────

The USS Maine *enters Havana Harbor in January 1898.*

move a friendly visit. In reality, its purpose was to protect U.S. interests and rescue Americans living in Cuba if war did break out.

The following month, the *New York Journal* printed a letter written by Enrique Dupuy de Lome, the Spanish minister in Washington. The letter, intended for a friend's eyes only, contained insulting statements about McKinley, calling him "weak and catering to the rabble." The New York press made the most out of the incident, calling it the "worst insult to the United States in its history." The letter caused a fierce public reaction in the United States against Spain.

REMEMBER THE *MAINE!*

Soon afterward, on February 15, 1898, a violent explosion ripped apart the battleship *Maine*. Two hundred sixty-six U.S. sailors died in the waters of Havana Harbor. The cause of the explosion was not known, but most Americans blamed Spain. Newspapers demanded war with Spain, and crowds chanted: "Remember the *Maine*! To hell with Spain!"

———————— ✧ ————————

The explosion of the USS Maine *inflamed anti-Spanish feelings throughout the United States.*

McKinley refused to panic. "I don't propose to be swept off my feet by the catastrophe," he said. "My duty is plain. We must learn the truth and endeavor, if possible, to fix the responsibility." He ordered a naval board of inquiry to investigate the cause of the explosion. For five weeks, they studied the remains of the ship and tried to determine the cause of the explosion. During those weeks, war fever grew in the United States.

While McKinley tried to find a diplomatic solution, he still saw war as a possibility and wanted the United States prepared. In early March, he asked Congress to set aside $50 million (more than $1 billion) for national defense. Congress approved the request and gave McKinley total control of the money. On March 25, the president received the naval commission's report. According to the report, the *Maine* explosion was caused by a submarine mine (an underwater explosive device), planted by unknown parties.

Later research proved the Spanish government had nothing to do with the sinking of the *Maine.* Historians believe it was an accident. There may have been an explosion in a coal storage room, some other type of accident aboard the ship, or a mine explosion. But in 1898, as Americans angrily mourned their lost sailors, they "knew" Spain had blown up the ship.

THE PRESSURE ON McKINLEY BUILDS

With tremendous pressure from all sides shouting for war, McKinley remained cautious. He worried about putting men's lives in danger. Remembering his days as a Civil War soldier, he said, "I have been through one war; I have seen the dead piled up; and I do not want to see another."

McKinley works at his desk in the Oval Office of the White House.

McKinley faced a lot of negative press for his restraint. Newspapers called him Wobbly Willie, and Theodore Roosevelt, his assistant secretary of the navy, accused him of having "a chocolate-eclair backbone."

In one last attempt to avoid war, McKinley sent a stern note to the Spanish government. He demanded an end to the fighting in Cuba and urged Spain to grant Cuba its independence. The Spanish government refused. By early April, McKinley realized his diplomatic efforts had failed. On April 11, he asked Congress for the authority to use military force in Cuba against Spain. "In the name of humanity, in the name of civilization, in behalf of endangered American interests which give us the right and the duty to speak and to act, the war in Cuba must stop," he said.

On April 24, 1898, Spain declared war on the United States. The next day, McKinley asked Congress to declare war on Spain. Congress did so, declaring that a state of war had existed with Spain since April 21. President McKinley, despite his efforts to prevent it, was now commander in chief of a war with Spain.

CHAPTER SEVEN

A WAR WITH SPAIN

Accepting war for humanity's sake, we must accept all obligations which the war in duty and honor imposes upon us. . . . Duty determines destiny.

—William McKinley, speech at the Citizens' Banquet, Chicago, October 19, 1898

The United States entered the Spanish-American War (1898) in a festive mood. Flags waved, bands played patriotic tunes, and young men stood in lines to volunteer. McKinley's first task as commander in chief was to equip the military for war. He ordered the navy to buy ships, massive supplies of coal, powder, and shells. As the regular army consisted of only 28,000 officers and soldiers, McKinley called for 125,000 volunteers. More than 1 million men flocked to the recruiting stations. Uniforms, tents, weapons, medical supplies, and large amounts of food had to be ordered. The army had to be trained. As these preparations for war began,

McKinley ordered the navy's Atlantic fleet to Havana, Cuba, to set up a blockade.

In 1898 the Philippines, a group of islands off the southeast coast of Asia, were the property of Spain. A group of Filipino rebels were also fighting for their independence. They wanted to free themselves from Spain's rule.

When the Spanish-American War began, most Americans, including President McKinley, had to pull out their maps to locate the Philippines. "I could not have told where those darned islands were within 2,000 miles," the president admitted.

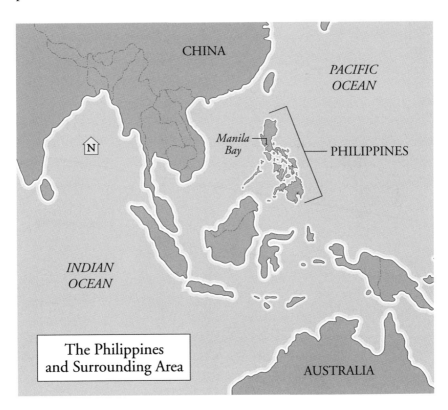

The Philippines and Surrounding Area

McKinley hoped to end the war quickly. Since a large portion of the Spanish fleet was in the Philippines, he sent Commodore George Dewey, commander of the Pacific fleet, to the Philippines. By destroying Spain's navy, McKinley would control the Pacific Ocean and prevent Spain from sending soldiers and supplies to Cuba.

THE FIRST MODERN PRESIDENT

President McKinley ran the war from the White House. He installed fifteen telephone lines that ran to his executive departments and Congress. He set up an early version of a voice recorder, called the graphophone, to leave messages and instructions for his aides. He turned an office in the southeastern corner of the White House into his War Room and installed twenty telegraph wires. Maps and

President McKinley set up this telegraph room in the White House to make plans and receive news about the Spanish-American War.

charts of Cuba and the Philippines covered the walls, and clerks recorded the movement of U.S. and Spanish forces. McKinley closely monitored all events.

The president also developed the first organized method for dealing with the press. He set up a long table on the second floor of the White House for reporters. McKinley's secretary spoke with them at noon and 4:00 P.M. daily. Reporters had greater access to the president than ever before.

"A SPLENDID LITTLE WAR"

The first battle of the war took place in the Philippines. McKinley ordered Commodore Dewey and his U.S. Navy Asiatic Squadron to capture or destroy the Spanish fleet in the Pacific Ocean. The battle took place at Manila Bay, the Philippines, on May 1, 1898. Dewey's fleet destroyed the entire Spanish naval force in the Philippines. None of the U.S. ships suffered major damage, and no Americans were killed in the battle.

Commodore George Dewey

The underwater telegraph cable had been cut during the battle, so the president did not hear of the victory until a week later. When he received the news, McKinley promoted Dewey to the rank of rear admiral and sent land troops to the island chain. He also sent a geologist to the Philippines to survey the islands' natural resources.

With a decisive victory in the Philippines, McKinley turned his attention to Cuba. In early June, he ordered U.S. army troops to set sail for the island. Seventeen thousand U.S. soldiers landed at the southeastern city of Daiquiri and marched fifteen miles westward toward Santiago. In early July, U.S. soldiers won major battles at El Caney, Kettle Hill, and San Juan Heights. While directing the war effort by telegraph from the War Room in the White House, McKinley pushed for the annexation of Hawaii. He signed a joint resolution annexing the islands on July 7.

Ten days later, the Spanish army in Santiago surrendered. When McKinley learned the terms of surrender, he thought they were too lenient. The Spanish soldiers offered to leave the city if the Americans allowed them to keep their weapons. McKinley wired an ultimatum that the arms must be surrendered. He offered to transport Spanish troops back to Spain. The Spanish officers agreed and lowered the Spanish flag. U.S. officers hoisted the Stars and Stripes up the flagpole on the roof of the governor's palace. The war was over.

Secretary of State John Hay called it "a splendid little war." But for U.S. soldiers, sweltering in Cuba's tropical heat, the end of the war couldn't come soon enough. They suffered from yellow fever, malaria, typhoid, diphtheria, and dysentery. Of the 5,500 men who died in the war, only 400 deaths were combat related. Disease claimed the rest.

NOW WHAT?

Queen Regent Maria Cristina of Spain sent a letter to President McKinley asking his conditions for peace. McKinley stated his terms. The Spaniards must leave Cuba and grant the Cuban people their independence. Spain must also cede (give up) Puerto Rico and Guam to the United States. McKinley would decide the fate of the Philippines at a later date. On October 1, representatives from Spain and the United States met in Paris, France, to work out the final details for peace.

For the next few months, McKinley wrestled with what to do about the Philippines. He faced pressure from political, military, and business groups to keep the islands. These groups believed in imperialism, the controlling of weaker nations by stronger nations. They looked to foreign lands as a way to expand U.S. power. Colonies could send raw materials to the United States and provide a market for U.S.-made goods. They also wanted to share the U.S. democratic form of government with other less-developed nations.

Another group of citizens, the Anti-Imperialist League, strongly disagreed with keeping the Philippines. They protested on moral grounds and held the opinion that obtaining colonies against the will of the people was wrong. The league included many prominent people, such as former President Grover Cleveland, author Mark Twain, and philanthropist Andrew Carnegie.

Andrew Carnegie

Carnegie wrote several newspaper and magazine articles protesting the retention of the Philippines. "Shall we hang in the school-houses of the Philippines our own

Declaration of Independence, and yet deny independence to them?" he asked in an article in the magazine *North American Review*. He also sent a stream of harshly critical letters to the president, cabinet members, and senators. In a letter to John Hay, Carnegie confided, "It is a great strain which the President is putting upon the loyalty of his friends and supporters. Many are bearing it—it has proved too great for me."

McKinley felt his role as president was to act on the wishes of the people. He listened to them and then shaped his policies to fit his perception of their wishes. In October 1898, he toured the midwestern and western United States to sound out public opinion on the Philippine question. In speech after speech, he urged unity, honor, and duty. "Wherever our flag floats, wherever we raise that standard of liberty, it is always for the sake of humanity and the advancement of civilization," he told a crowd in Chariton, Iowa. "Territory sometimes comes to us when we go to war in a holy cause, and whenever it does the banner of liberty will float over it and bring, I trust, blessings and benefits to all the people." The great applause that greeted his words assured McKinley that most Americans favored acquiring the Philippines.

In the end, McKinley decided the Filipinos needed U.S. protection and guidance. Since the vast majority of the Filipino population was uneducated, the president believed they were incapable of self-government. He also feared other colonial powers, such as Germany and Japan, would take possession of the islands if the United States left the area. "There was nothing left for us to do but to take them all, and to educate the Filipinos, and uplift them and civilize and Christianize them, and by God's grace do the very best we could by them," he said.

THE IMPERIALISM PROBLEM

When the Spanish-American War ended, the United States purchased the Philippines from Spain. President McKinley's plan to civilize and Christianize the Filipinos before granting them independence brought with it a host of questions never before faced by a U.S. president. Should the Filipinos be given all the rights of U.S. citizens? Limited rights? Did the Constitution apply to them? What responsibilities did the Filipinos have to the United States?

"It is sometimes hard to determine what is best to do, and the best thing to do is oftentimes the hardest," McKinley said as he considered these questions. He appointed a commission to go to Manila, gather information, and recommend a policy for administering the islands. The commission members listened to people from every field. They found the Filipino people "had great potential for self-rule and full development, were bright, engaging, and quick to learn, but it would be years before they could successfully grapple with the problems of government."

McKinley wanted to establish a civil government and gradually train the native people to administer that government on their own. When they proved capable of self-rule, U.S. involvement would end. His commission outlined a plan for a Philippine government. The plan called for an executive branch, a legislature, and a cabinet. The president appointed William Howard Taft governor-general, or head of the executive branch of the new government.

In the spring of 1901, the U.S. Supreme Court declared the Philippines were U.S. dependencies, subject to congressional authority. The Filipino people were given civil rights, but not full U.S. citizenship. Finally, on July 4, 1946, the Philippines gained their full independence.

The Treaty of Paris was signed on December 10, 1898, and ratified (approved) by the U.S. Senate the following February. Cuba became an independent nation. Spain gave Puerto Rico and Guam to the United States as payment for fighting the war. The United States bought the Philippines from Spain for $20 million ($408 million).

TROUBLE IN THE PHILIPPINES

McKinley's problems in the Philippines didn't end with the signing of the peace treaty. The Filipinos had expected to be granted freedom, like Cuba. They felt betrayed when they learned they had traded one ruler for another. They resented the United States as much as they had Spain. General Emilio Aguinaldo led attacks against U.S. soldiers in the Philippines. By the end of 1899, McKinley had sent more than 60,000 U.S. troops to suppress the fighting on the islands. The Philippine Insurrection was a brutal war. Both sides committed unspeakable cruelty and senseless violence.

To restore peace and create a civil government, McKinley again sent William Howard Taft to the islands. The president instructed Taft to set up municipal governments and bring the Filipinos "the blessings of peace and liberty." The Taft Commission modified the tax system, reorganized the local police, and built village schools. They also arranged for garbage disposal and introduced health programs to control deadly diseases such as cholera, malaria, and smallpox.

As the nineteenth century came to an end, McKinley thought about his future. He purchased his old home in Canton, Ohio, and looked forward to retirement. His vice president, Garret Hobart, died in November 1899. McKinley mourned his friend and adviser. Republican leaders

President McKinley and Vice President Garrett Hobart pose
for a photograph shortly before Hobart's death.

approached him about running for a second term. "I would be the happiest man in America if I could go out of office in 1901." he said. "There is only one condition upon which I would listen to such a suggestion, and that is, a perfectly clear and imperative call of duty."

CHAPTER EIGHT

FOUR MORE YEARS OF THE FULL DINNER PAIL

We have not only been successful in our financial and business affairs, but in a war with a foreign power which has added great glory to American arms and a new chapter to American History.

—William McKinley, speech at the Home Market Club, Boston, February 16, 1899

Foreign affairs continued to dominate President McKinley's time and attention as the twentieth century began. The Spanish-American War was over, but the president still found himself dealing with problems outside U.S. borders.

LET'S BUILD A CANAL

During the war, ships traveling between the Atlantic Ocean and the Pacific Ocean had to steam thousands of miles around the southern tip of South America. McKinley, along

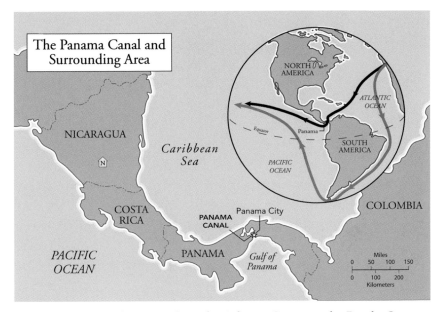

The inset shows the routes from the Atlantic Ocean to the Pacific Ocean before (grey line) *and after* (black line) *the Panama Canal was built.*

with most Americans, saw the need for a shortcut. A canal—a humanmade waterway—in Central America would connect the two oceans. A treaty between the United States and Great Britain, however, stated that neither country could build a canal without the cooperation of the other. President McKinley and Secretary of State Hay began talks with Great Britain for the rights to build a canal in Central America.

McKinley appointed a canal commission to investigate the best location for the site. Some people favored a canal across Nicaragua, others a route across Panama. The president urged Hay to write a new treaty with the British ambassador, Sir Julian Pauncefote. The two diplomats created the Hay-Pauncefote Treaty. The agreement permitted the United States to build a canal that would be open to all vessels in peace and war. McKinley sent the treaty to the Senate for approval, calling it a "great achievement."

McKinley and Hay were shocked when the majority of senators opposed the treaty. Hay grew depressed, thinking he had failed the president. After a cabinet meeting, Hay handed McKinley a sealed envelope. The president absently put the envelope in his pocket. When he opened the envelope hours later, he found Hay's resignation. McKinley refused to accept it. He returned the resignation and wrote his secretary of state an encouraging letter. "Had I known the contents of the letter which you handed me this morning, I would have declined to receive or consider it," he began. "Nothing could be more

✧ ——————————
John Hay was U.S. secretary of state for seven years.

unfortunate than to have you retire from the cabinet. The personal loss would be great, but the public loss even greater." He signed the letter, "Yours devotedly, William McKinley." Hay stayed on as secretary of state and continued to work on a second Hay-Pauncefote Treaty. It eventually passed the U.S. Senate and led to the building of the Panama Canal.

AN OPEN DOOR TO CHINA

Another foreign policy problem surfaced for McKinley, this time in China. Everyone wanted a piece of the rich China trade. Great Britain, Germany, Russia, France, and Japan carved China into commercial regions called spheres of influence. Each country held commercial dominance within their region. McKinley wanted to keep China intact. He also wanted to create new markets for U.S. products and keep U.S. workers busy. His motto became, "Regular employment, good wages, and education bring prosperity and happiness."

Secretary of State Hay pushed for an open door policy. This plan called for all nations to trade with China on an equal basis. Harbor dues and railroad rates (payment for the use of harbors and railroads) would be the same for all. McKinley explained the policy to the American public. "It is just to use every legitimate means for the enlargement of American trade; but we seek no advantages in the Orient which are not common to all. Asking only the open door for ourselves, we are ready to accord the open door to others." On March 20, 1900, Hay announced that the other nations involved had accepted the Open Door Policy. The United States considered it the "final and definitive" word on China trade, even though the Chinese had not been involved in the discussions.

McKinley achieved another major goal in March. The House of Representatives passed a bill declaring gold the official standard of U.S. currency. McKinley signed the Gold Standard Act into law with a special gold pen given to him by a group of statesmen. Satisfied with his accomplishments and anxious to escape the summer heat, President McKinley and Ida left Washington to spend the summer at their home in Canton, Ohio.

THE BOXER REBELLION

Relaxation was not an option for the president, however. By early summer, a group of Chinese fighters called the Righteous and Harmonious Fists rose up against outside

Boxers traveled along the Grand Canal to reach the parts of China where foreign settlements were located.

interference in China. The group, called Boxers by western-ers, hated foreigners and wanted them to leave their coun-try. The Chinese empress secretly supported the Boxers and ordered all foreigners killed. The Boxers succeeded in killing many foreigners and Chinese Christians. In June the Boxers rioted in the city of Beijing, burned foreign proper-ty, and held a group of foreigners hostage.

McKinley kept a close watch on the situation in China and communicated with his cabinet by telephone. The last thing he wanted to do was send troops, but clearly, some-thing had to be done to protect Americans in China. In August 1900, the president sent 2,100 U.S. soldiers to join Japanese, Russian, British, and French troops. The interna-tional force fought its way to Beijing, freed the captives, and put down the rebellion.

CHOOSING A VICE PRESIDENT

McKinley enjoyed the quiet of Canton and the peacefulness of his cozy home. He had accomplished much in the few short years he'd been in office. The economy was flourish-ing. He had won a war and turned the United States into a global power. Although small battles still took place in the Philippines, peace and a stable democratic government were just around the corner. McKinley talked about stepping down after his first term but wanted to complete the work he started. "We have been moving in untried paths," he said, "but our steps have been guided by honor and duty. There will be no turning aside, no wavering, no retreat."

The real question was not whether McKinley would run again but who he would choose as his running mate. McKinley considered several men for vice president, but his initial choices turned him down. Spanish-American War hero and governor of New York Theodore Roosevelt carried strong support, but he didn't want the position either. "I am not going to take it on any account," he said of the vice presidency. "It is the very last office I would want or care for."

Support for Roosevelt grew. Mark Hanna, McKinley's campaign manager, disliked and distrusted Roosevelt. The two men clashed on many issues. Hanna did everything he could to prevent Roosevelt from becoming vice president. "Don't you understand that there is just one life between this crazy man and the presidency?" Hanna exclaimed.

McKinley decided to let the Republican convention decide on the vice-presidential candidate. Roosevelt agreed. If the convention nominated him, he would accept.

Mark Hanna
——————— ◇ ———————

The convention met in Philadelphia. When Senator Joseph B. Foraker of Ohio nominated McKinley as the Republican presidential candidate, a tidal wave of cheers erupted on the convention floor. With shouts of "Teddy! Teddy! Teddy!" the convention chose Theodore Roosevelt

Voters at the Republican convention in 1900 called on Theodore Roosevelt to run for vice president alongside McKinley.

✧ ————————

for vice president. Mark Hanna grumbled but accepted the party's choice. "Your *duty* to the Country is to *live* for four years from next March," he wrote to McKinley.

AN ANARCHIST PLOT

Mark Hanna's comment may have stemmed from worry over McKinley's safety. A secret service agent had uncovered a plot to assassinate six world leaders, including McKinley. Anarchists, people who are against any form of government, had already murdered Empress Elizabeth of Austria. Then, on July 29, King Humbert I of Italy was shot and killed at his summer palace. Those closest to McKinley urged him to cut back his schedule and take more safety precautions.

The president ignored them saying, "I have no enemies. Why should I fear?"

THE 1900 PRESIDENTIAL CAMPAIGN

The Democrats chose William Jennings Bryan as their presidential candidate. Imperialism became the dominant issue of the 1900 campaign. Bryan described McKinley as a greedy expansionist bent on grabbing land all over the globe and oppressing the natives to benefit U.S. big business. He brutally attacked McKinley's character and his first term as president. McKinley calmly stayed in Canton. He

✧ ————————
William Jennings Bryan was McKinley's presidential opponent for the second time in 1900.

McKinley, pictured here with Ida, campaigned from the porch of his home in Canton, Ohio.

───────── ✧

felt it was improper for a president to campaign for reelection while in office. Mark Hanna plastered the country with McKinley posters, buttons, and pamphlets. Roosevelt also traveled around the country and campaigned for the McKinley-Roosevelt team.

McKinley won the election by a greater majority than he had in 1896. The victory was particularly sweet, as it assured the president of the country's faith in him and his first administration. "I can no longer be called the President of a party," he said. "I am now the President of the whole people."

McKinley (standing center, second from right) *takes the oath of office for the second time.*

CHAPTER NINE

A TRIP TO BUFFALO

*Let us keep always in mind that the
foundation of our Government is liberty;
its superstructure peace.*

—William McKinley's fourth State of the Union
message, December 3, 1900

On March 4, 1901, William McKinley took his second oath of office as president of the United States in a drenching rain. A huge crowd stood under umbrellas to listen to his acceptance speech. He spoke of the strong economy and his desire to enlarge foreign markets for U.S. goods. He talked about the Philippines and pledged to continue his efforts to establish a democratic government there. The nasty weather did not dampen the cheers. McKinley started his second term on a wave of popular approval.

Since the country was flourishing and no crisis loomed on the horizon, McKinley decided to take a six-week trip across the United States. He wanted to see the people and sound out public opinion on his ideas for expanding foreign trade. He planned to leave Washington at the end of April and travel by train through the South to the Pacific coast. The return trip would take a northern route and end up at the Pan-American Exposition in Buffalo, New York.

On April 29, the president and his wife—along with cabinet members and their wives, invited guests, and newspaper reporters—boarded the presidential train and set out on their cross-country adventure. Cheering crowds met the presidential party at every stop. In El Paso, Texas, Ida developed a felon, or infection, on her fingertip. Her doctor cut open the felon to relieve Ida's pain. The train proceeded across the country.

Enormous crowds met the president in Los Angeles, California. Six white horses pulled his carriage, which was covered with flowers. Rose petals poured down on him as he stood in the reviewing stand and waved to the people.

✧ —————

McKinley rides in a carriage covered with roses during his tour of California.

As one reporter noted, "No President—certainly no president since the days of Lincoln—has been so close to the hearts of the people as Mr. McKinley."

Ida did her best to keep up during the constant festivities. On the way to San Francisco, her doctor halted the train and lanced her infected finger again. She developed a high fever, a blood infection, and an inflammation in the lining of her heart. She was rushed to San Francisco for treatment and rest. McKinley canceled his schedule and stayed by his wife's side. She grew progressively worse.

By May 15, newspaper reports called her illness critical and speculated that she would not recover. McKinley arranged for a funeral train to carry her back to Washington. He sat by her sickbed, day and night. News of his devotion swept across the nation. As Ida hovered between life and death, McKinley's popularity surged to an all-time high.

Then, suddenly, Ida rallied. She regained consciousness and began to improve. McKinley left the sickroom for short intervals and made several public appearances. When Ida was well enough to travel, they began the trip back to Washington. McKinley canceled his visit to the Pan-American Exposition. He promised to reschedule it later in the year.

McKinley's popularity caused some Republican leaders to discuss the possibility of his running for a third term. The president wasted no time ending the speculation. He issued a statement to the press and announced he would not run for a third term under any circumstances. In early July, he and Ida went home to Canton so Ida could continue her recovery.

McKinley installed a temporary executive office in the library of his North Market Street home. As Ida grew stronger, the president conducted business and enjoyed the

slower pace of life in Canton. He and his secretary, George
Cortelyou, planned his visit to the Pan-American Exposition
in September. As they worked out McKinley's schedule,
Cortelyou canceled a reception scheduled at the Temple of
Music. He thought it would be difficult to protect the president with thousands of people milling around. But McKinley
wanted to greet the people and shake their hands. He put
the reception back on the schedule saying, "No one would
wish to hurt me." Twice, Cortelyou removed the reception
from the itinerary. Twice, McKinley put it back on.

THE PAN-AMERICAN EXPOSITION

September 5, 1901, was dubbed President's Day at the Pan-
American Exposition in Buffalo, New York. The McKinleys
arrived in an open car-
riage. They marveled at
the gleaming domes,
glistening fountains,
and new inventions on
display. McKinley thor-
oughly enjoyed viewing
Thomas Edison's new
wireless telegraph and
the 375-foot electric
tower powered by the
waters of Niagara Falls.

——————— ✧

*Edison's electric tower lit
up the sky of Buffalo,
New York.*

McKinley (center left, walking up the stairs) *visits Niagara Falls.*

———————————— ✧ ————————————

The president gave what historians consider the greatest speech of his life before 50,000 people. He urged greater participation by the United States in world affairs, saying, "Isolation is no longer possible or desirable." That night, he and Ida watched a fireworks display and stayed in the home of John Milburn, president of the exposition. The next morning, they visited Niagara Falls.

After their visit to the falls, Ida returned to the Milburn house to rest. McKinley waved good-bye to his wife and proceeded to the reception at the Temple of Music. Just after 4:00 P.M. twenty-eight-year-old Leon Czolgosz, an anarchist, stood face-to-face with McKinley in the receiving line. Czolgosz fired two rounds from his Iver-Johnson revolver into the president.

*McKinley was shot by Leon Czolgosz on
September 6, 1901, in Buffalo, New York.*

———————————————— ✧ ————————————————

Czolgosz shot McKinley on Friday afternoon. Throughout
the weekend, Vice President Roosevelt, cabinet members,
friends, and relatives waited anxiously for updates from
McKinley's doctors. Ida wanted to stay by her husband's side,
but his doctors only granted her short visits. By Monday the
president seemed to improve. His temperature had gone
down. His spirits were good, his mind clear.

By Wednesday, September 11, McKinley felt well
enough to ask for solid food and a cigar. They gave him the
food, not the cigar. His doctors confidently announced that
the president would recover and declared him "out of danger." Vice President Roosevelt left for a wilderness vacation
in the Adirondack Mountains. Several cabinet members
returned to Washington. The president, used to having lots
of people around, told Cortelyou he was getting lonesome.

The next day, he suffered a relapse. Gangrene (decay) had set in along the path of the bullet in McKinley's stomach, pancreas, and kidneys. His fever rose, and infection ravaged his body. His physicians realized he was dying.

Surrounded by family and friends, McKinley said good-bye to those he loved. He put his arm around Ida and smiled at her. "It is God's way; His will, not ours, be done," he said. In his last moments, he repeated a portion of the hymn "Nearer, my God, to Thee." He died early Saturday morning, September 14, 1901, eight days after being shot.

Vice President Roosevelt rushed back from his vacation and took the oath of office. "It shall be my aim to

——————————— ✧ ———————————

Theodore Roosevelt was sworn in as president
at the Wilcox house in Buffalo, New York.

continue absolutely unbroken the policy of President McKinley for the peace and prosperity and honor of our beloved country," he promised.

Funeral services for McKinley were held in Buffalo, Washington, and Canton. Bells tolled, flags flew at half-mast, and the nation grieved. "There have undoubtedly been greater and stronger Presidents than he was," said politician George McClellan Jr., "but none was a more kindly nor a more courteous gentleman, and none has died more regretted by his countrymen, nor more beloved."

Leon Czolgosz's trial began nine days after McKinley's death. He admitted he was an anarchist. The jury found

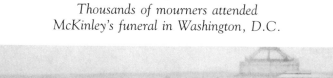

Thousands of mourners attended McKinley's funeral in Washington, D.C.

him guilty and sentenced him to death. He was executed by electric chair on October 29.

Ida McKinley lived the rest of her life in Canton. Her younger sister cared for her. Ida visited her husband's grave almost daily. According to friends and family members, she never again suffered from seizures. Ida died in 1907 and was buried beside McKinley in Canton.

A LASTING LEGACY

William McKinley was a devout Christian, a devoted husband, and a kind man. He spent his life serving the country he loved, always doing what he perceived was best for it. Bit by bit, he strengthened and broadened the power of the president. He greatly expanded the U.S. role in international affairs and led the United States into the twentieth century as a world power.

In his memorial address of President McKinley, Secretary of State John Hay said, "The Republic grieved over such a son, but is proud forever of having produced him. After all, in spite of its tragic ending, his life was extraordinarily happy. He had, all his days, troops of friends, the cheer of fame and fruitful labor."

Timeline

1843 William McKinley is born on January 29 in Niles, Ohio.

1852 McKinley's family moves to Poland, Ohio. William attends Poland Academy.

1860 McKinley attends Allegheny College in Meadville, Pennsylvania.

1861 McKinley teaches school and works at the post office in Poland, Ohio. Confederate forces attack Fort Sumter, South Carolina, starting the Civil War. McKinley joins the 23rd Regiment, Ohio Volunteer Infantry in the Union army.

1862 McKinley is promoted to commissary sergeant. He distinguishes himself at the Battle of Antietam and is promoted to second lieutenant.

1863 McKinley is promoted to first lieutenant.

1864 McKinley is promoted to captain.

1865 McKinley is promoted to brevet major. The Civil War ends. McKinley returns to Poland, Ohio, and works in the law office of Judge Charles Glidden.

1866 McKinley attends Albany Law School in Albany, New York.

1867 McKinley is admitted to the Ohio Bar Association and sets up a law practice in Canton, Ohio.

1869 McKinley is elected county prosecutor for Stark County, Ohio.

1871 McKinley marries Ida Saxton on January 25. He runs for reelection as county prosecutor and loses. Daughter Katherine is born on December 25.

1873 Daughter Ida is born and dies four months later.

1875 Daughter Katherine dies of typhoid fever.

1876 McKinley is elected to the U.S. House of Representatives from the Eighteenth Congressional District of Ohio.

1878 McKinley wins reelection to a second term in Congress.

1880 McKinley wins reelection to a third term in Congress and is appointed to the House Ways and Means Committee.

1882 McKinley wins reelection to a fourth term in Congress by a narrow majority. Democratic candidate Jonathan Wallace contests the election results.

1884 In May a congressional committee votes to give McKinley's House seat to Wallace. In November, McKinley runs for reelection and wins a fifth term in Congress.

1886 McKinley wins reelection to a sixth term in Congress.

1888 McKinley wins reelection to a seventh term in Congress.

1889 McKinley becomes chairman of the House Ways and Means Committee.

1890 McKinley writes and sponsors the McKinley Tariff legislation and is defeated in his bid for reelection to Congress.

1891 McKinley is elected governor of Ohio.

1893 McKinley wins reelection as governor of Ohio.

1896 McKinley is elected president of the United States.

1898 The battleship *Maine* explodes and sinks in Havana Harbor. The United States declares war on Spain. McKinley signs a congressional resolution annexing the Hawaiian Islands. The Spanish-American War ends. Cuba becomes an independent nation. Spain gives Puerto Rico and Guam to the United States. The United States purchases the Philippine Islands from Spain for $20 million.

1899 McKinley asks Secretary of State John Hay to issue the Open Door policy toward China.

1900 The Boxer Rebellion against foreigners in China begins. McKinley runs for reelection with Theodore Roosevelt as his running mate. His opponent is William Jennings Bryan. McKinley defeats Bryan.

1901 McKinley is shot by anarchist Leon Czolgosz in Buffalo, New York, on September 6. McKinley dies due to infection of his wounds on September 14.

1907 McKinley's wife, Ida, dies in Canton, Ohio.

SOURCE NOTES

7 Marshall Everett, *Complete Life of William McKinley and Story of His Assassination* (United States: Marshall Everett, 1901), 120.

8 Charles S. Olcott, *The Life of William McKinley: Vol. 2* (Boston: Houghton Mifflin Company, 1916), 316.

8 Ibid., 316.

10 Emil P. Herbruck, *Early Years and Late Reflections* (Cleveland, OH: Central Publishing House, 1923), 218.

11 Charles S. Olcott, *The Life of William McKinley: Vol. 1* (Boston: Houghton Mifflin Company, 1916), 6.

11 Joseph G. Butler Jr., *Recollections of Men and Events* (New York: G. P. Putnam's Sons, 1925), 23.

13 Joseph G. Butler Jr., *Life of William McKinley and History of National McKinley Birthplace Memorial* (Cleveland: Joseph G. Butler, Jr., 1924), 5.

13 Ibid., 6.

13 Margaret Leech, *In the Days of McKinley* (New York: Harper & Brothers, 1959), 5.

14 Robert P. Porter, *Life of William McKinley, Soldier, Lawyer, Statesman* (Cleveland, OH: N. G. Hamilton Publishing Company, 1896), 40.

14 William H. Armstrong, *Major McKinley: William McKinley and the Civil War* (Kent, OH: Kent State University Press, 2000), 7.

17 Ibid., 10.

19 Charles Richard Williams, ed., *The Diary and Letters of Rutherford B. Hayes, Nineteenth President of the United States, Vol. 2* (Columbus, OH: Ohio State Archaeological and Historical Society, 1922), 533.

19 "Our Army Correspondence: Letter from One of the Poland Boys," *Mahoning Register*, Youngstown, OH, June 27, 1861.

20 H. Wayne Morgan, ed., "A Civil War Diary of William McKinley," *The Ohio Historical Quarterly*, Vol. 69 (1960), 277.

20 Ibid., 288.

20 William McKinley, *Speeches and Addresses of William McKinley from His Election to Congress to the Present Time* (New York: D. Appleton and Company, 1893), 643.

21 Porter, *Life of William McKinley*, 47.

21 Armstrong, *Major McKinley*, 32.

22 H. Wayne Morgan, *William McKinley and His America* (Syracuse, NY: Syracuse University Press, 1963), 25.

22 Porter, *Life of William McKinley*, 48.

23 Murat Halstead, *The Illustrious Life of William McKinley, Our Martyred President* (Chicago: Murat Halstead, 1901), 31–32.

24 Alexander K. McClure and Charles Morris, *The Authentic Life of William McKinley: Our Third Martyr President* (Philadelphia: W. E. Scull, 1901), 91.

25 Murat Halstead, *Life and Distinguished Services of William McKinley, Our Martyr President* (Chicago: M. A. Donohue & Company, 1901), 54.

27 "Major Wm. McKinley," *Canton* (OH) *Repository and Republican*, Canton, Ohio, October 7, 1869.

28 Olcott, *The Life of William McKinley, Vol. 1*, 57.

28 Ibid., 57–58.

29 Ibid., 60.
32 Porter, *Life of William McKinley*, 111.
33 Thomas Beer, *Hanna* (New York: Alfred A. Knopf, 1929), 102.
34 Beer, *Hanna*, 103.
37 Ibid., 110.
38 Porter, *Life of William McKinley*, 138.
39 McKinley, *Speeches and Address of William McKinley from His Election to Congress to the Present Time*, 117.
39 Ibid., 25.
40 Olcott, *The Life of William McKinley: Vol. 2*, 360–361.
40 Ibid., 359.
43 Robert La Follette, *La Follette's Autobiography* (Madison, WI: University of Wisconsin Press, 1911), 58.
43 Ibid., 42.
43–44 McKinley, *Speeches and Addresses of William McKinley from His Election to Congress to the Present Time*, 336.
44 Ibid., 430.
47 "In Open Air, Governor McKinley Takes the Oath in Bright Sunshine," *Daily* (Columbus) *Ohio State Journal*, January 9, 1894.
47 McKinley, *Speeches and Addresses of William McKinley from His Election to Congress to the Present Time*, 523.
50 Olcott, *The Life of William McKinley: Volume I*, 291.
50 Morgan, *William McKinley and His America*, 177.
51 Leech, *In the Days of McKinley*, 63.
52 Colonel T. Bentley Mott, *Myron T. Herrick: Friend of France* (Garden City, NY: Doubleday, Doran & Company, 1929), 61.
52 "McKinley's Nomination Probable," *Brooklyn* (NY) *Daily Eagle*, May 1, 1896.
53 Mott, *Myron T. Herrick*, 64.
54 Charles G. Dawes, *A Journal of the McKinley Years* (Chicago: Lakeside Press, 1950), 89.
57 Beer, *Hanna*, 165.
57 Herman H. Kohlsaat, *From McKinley to Harding: Personal Recollections of Our Presidents* (New York: Charles Scribner's Sons, 1923), 54.
58 William McKinley, *Speeches and Addresses of William McKinley: From March 1, 1897 to May 30, 1900* (New York: Doubleday & McClure Co., 1900), 12.
58 Ibid., 1.
60 Olcott, *The Life of William McKinley: Vol. 2*, 346.
62 H. Wayne Morgan, *America's Road to Empire: The War with Spain and Overseas Expansion* (New York: John Wiley and Sons, 1967), 25.
62 William McKinley, "William McKinley: First Annual Message," American Presidency Project: University of California, Santa Barbara, Department of Political Science, N.d., <http://www.presidency.ucsb.edu/ws/index.php?pid=29538> (June 22, 2004).
64 Charles H. Brown, *The Correspondents' War: Journalists in the Spanish-American War* (New York: Charles Scribner's Sons, 1967), 113.
64 Ibid., 112.
64 Art Young, *Art Young: His Life and Times* (New York: Sheridan House, 1939), 196.
65 Olcott, *The Life of William McKinley, Vol. 2*, 12.

65 Hermann Hagedorn, *Leonard Wood, Vol. I* (New York: Harper & Brothers Publishers, 1931), 141.

66 Kohlsaat, *From McKinley to Harding*, 77.

66–67 "William McKinley: War Message, April 11, 1898," Encyclopedia Britannica Online, N.d., <http://www.britannica.com/eb/article-9116941> (June 22, 2006).

68 McKinley, *Speeches and Addresses of William McKinley from March 1, 1897 to May 30, 1900*, 134.

69 Kohlsaat, *From McKinley to Harding*, 68.

72 Frank Freidel, *The Splendid Little War* (Boston: Little, Brown and Company, 1958), 3.

73–74 Andrew Carnegie, *The Gospel of Wealth and Other Timely Essays* (1900; reprint, Cambridge, MA: The Belknap Press of Harvard University Press, 1962), 129.

74 Letter from Andrew Carnegie to John Hay, November 24, 1898, Andrew Carnegie Papers, Vol. 57, Library of Congress.

74 McKinley, *Speeches and Addresses of William McKinley from March 1, 1897 to May 30, 1900*, 114.

74 Leech, *In the Days of McKinley*, 345.

75 McKinley, *Speeches and Addresses of William McKinley from March 1, 1897 to May 30, 1900*, 190.

75 Morgan, *William McKinley and His America*, 443.

76 Olcott, *The Life of William McKinley: Vol. 2*, 177.

77 Ibid., 307.

78 McKinley, *Speeches and Addresses of William McKinley from March 1, 1897 to May 30, 1900*, 185.

80 Leech, *In the Days of McKinley*, 508.

80–81 William Roscoe Thayer, *The Life and Letters of John Hay: Vol. 2* (Boston: Houghton Mifflin Company, 1929), 227–228.

81 Kohlsaat, *From McKinley to Harding*, 72.

81 Lewis L. Gould, *The Presidency of William McKinley* (Lawrence: University Press of Kansas, 1980), 201.

83 Halstead, *The Illustrious Life of William McKinley*, 180–181.

84 Kohlsaat, *From McKinley to Harding*, 86.

84 Beer, Hanna, 236.

84 Halstead, *The Illustrious Life of William McKinley*, 162.

85 Leech, *In the Days of McKinley*, 542.

86 Ibid., 584.

87 Olcott, *The Life of William McKinley: Volume II*, 296.

89 "William McKinley: Fourth Annual Message," American Presidency Project: University of California, Santa Barbara, Department of Political Science, <http://www.presidency.ucsb.edu/ws/index.php?pid=29541> (June 22, 2006).

91 Henry Litchfield West, "The President's Recent Tour," *The Forum*, 31, August 1901, 668–669.

92 Olcott, *The Life of William McKinley: Volume II*, 314.

93 Everett, *Complete Life of William McKinley and Story of His Assassination*, 116.

94 "Doctors Have No Fear,"
Washington Post, Wednesday,
September 11, 1901.

95 Dawes, *A Journal of the McKinley
Years*, 280.

95 Kohlsaat, *From McKinley to
Harding*, 95.

96 "The New President," *Washington
Post*, Sunday, September 15, 1901.

96 Harold C. Syrett, ed., *The
Gentleman and the Tiger: The
Autobiography of George B.
McClellan, Jr.* (Philadelphia: J. B.
Lippincott Company, 1956), 121.

97 John Hay, *Memorial Address on the
Life and Character of William
McKinley* (Washington, D.C.:
Government Printing Office, 1903),
49–50.

SELECTED BIBLIOGRAPHY

Armstrong, William H. *Major McKinley: William McKinley and the Civil War*. Kent, OH: Kent State University Press, 2000.

Beer, Thomas. *Hanna*. New York: Alfred A. Knopf, 1929.

Brown, Charles H. *The Correspondents' War: Journalists in the Spanish-American War*. New York: Charles Scribner's Sons, 1967.

Butler, Joseph G. Jr. *Life of William McKinley and History of National McKinley Birthplace Memorial*. Cleveland, OH: Joseph G. Butler Jr., 1924.

Butler, Joseph G. Jr. *Recollections of Men and Events*. New York: G. P. Putnam's Sons, 1925.

Dawes, Charles, G. *A Journal of the McKinley Years*. Chicago: The Lakeside Press, 1950.

Everett, Marshall. *Complete Life of William McKinley and Story of His Assassination*. United States: Marshall Everett, 1901.

Freidel, Frank. *The Splendid Little War*. Boston: Little, Brown and Company, 1958.

Gould, Lewis L. *The Presidency of William McKinley*. Lawrence, Ks: University Press of Kansas, 1980.

Halstead, Murat. *The Illustrious Life of William McKinley, Our Martyred President*. Chicago: Murat Halstead, 1901.

Herbruck, Emil P. *Early Years and Late Reflections*. Cleveland, OH: Central Publishing House, 1923.

Kohlsaat, Herman. H. *From McKinley to Harding: Personal Recollections of Our Presidents*. New York: Charles Scribner's Sons, 1923.

La Follette, Robert. *La Follette's Autobiography*. Madison, WI: The University of Wisconsin Press, 1911.

Leech, Margaret. *In the Days of McKinley*. New York: Harper & Brothers, 1959.

McClure, Alexander K., and Charles Morris. *The Authentic Life of William McKinley: Our Third Martyr President*. Philadelphia: W. E. Scull, 1901.

McKinley, William. *Speeches and Addresses of William McKinley from His Election to Congress to the Present Time*. New York: D. Appleton and Company, 1893.

McKinley, William. *Speeches and Addresses of William McKinley from March 1, 1897 to May 30, 1900*. New York: Doubleday & McClure Co., 1900.

Morgan, H. Wayne. *America's Road to Empire: The War with Spain and Overseas Expansion*. New York: John Wiley and Sons, 1967.

Morgan, H. Wayne. *William McKinley and His America*. Syracuse, NY: Syracuse University Press, 1963.

Morgan, H. Wayne, ed. "A Civil War Diary of William McKinley," *The Ohio Historical Quarterly*, Volume 69, 1960.

Mott, Colonel T. Bentley. *Myron T. Herrick: Friend of France*. Garden City, NY: Doubleday, Doran & Company, 1929.

Olcott, Charles S. *The Life of William McKinley: Volumes I & II*. Boston: Houghton Mifflin Company, 1916.

Porter, Robert P. *Life of William McKinley, Soldier, Lawyer, Statesman*. Cleveland, OH: N. G. Hamilton Publishing Company, 1896.

Thayer, William Roscoe. *The Life and Letters of John Hay: Volumes I & II*. Boston: Houghton Mifflin Company, 1929.

Further Reading and Websites

American President.org: William McKinley (1897–1901): 25th President of the United States
http://www.americanpresident.org/history/williammckinley
This website lists important facts about McKinley and also features a brief biography.

Barber, James, and Amy Pastan. *Presidents and First Ladies*. New York: DK Publishing, 2002.

Bausum, Ann. *Our Country's Presidents*. Washington, DC: National Geographic Society, 2001.

Blue, Rose, and Corinne J. Naden. *The Expansion Years: 1857 to 1901*. Austin, TX: Raintree Steck-Vaughn Publishers, 1998.

Collins, David R. *William McKinley: 25th President of the United States*. Ada, OK: Garrett Educational Corporation, 1990.

Dolan, Edward F. *The Spanish-American War*. Minneapolis: Millbrook Press, 2001.

DuTemple, Lesley A. *The Panama Canal*. Minneapolis: Twenty-First Century Books, 2003.

Gay, Kathlyn, and Martin Gay. *Spanish-American War*. Minneapolis: Twenty-First Century Books, 1995.

Golay, Michael. *Spanish-American War*. New York: Facts on File, 2003.

Goldman, David J. *Presidential Losers*. Minneapolis: Lerner Publications Company, 2004.

Green, Carl R. *The Spanish-American War*. Berkeley Heights, NJ: Enslow Publishers, 2002.

Jones, Rebecca C. *The President Has Been Shot! True Stories of the Attacks on Ten U.S. Presidents*. New York: Dutton Children's Books, 1996.

Klingel, Cynthia A., and Robert B. Noyed. *William McKinley: Our Twenty-Fifth President*. Chanhassen, MN: The Child's World, 2002.

Marrin, Albert. *The Spanish-American War*. New York: Atheneum, 1991.

McKinley Memorial Library and Museum
http://www.mckinley.lib.oh.us
The McKinley Library and Museum website includes information about the president and his presidency.

McPherson, Stephanie Sammartino. *Theodore Roosevelt*. Minneapolis: Twenty-First Century Books, 2005.

Naval Historical Center Home Page: Spanish-American War
http://www.history.navy.mil/photos/events/spanam/eve-pge.htm
This site features links to historical photographs and illustrations from the U.S. Navy Historical Center archives.

New York Public Library Online Exhibition of the Spanish-American War
http://www.nypl.org/research/chss/epo/spanexhib
Learn more about the Spanish American War from this retrospective website created by the New York Public Library.

PBS.org: Crucible of Empire: The Spanish-American War
http://www.pbs.org/crucible
This is a companion site to the PBS documentary about the Spanish-American War.

PresidentsUSA.net: William McKinley
http://www.presidentsusa.net/mckinley.html
This website has information about McKinley, as well as many helpful links to other resources about McKinley.

Robinson, Mary Alice Burke, ed. *The Spanish-American War: America Emerges as a World Power*. Carlisle, MA: Discovery Enterprises, 1998.

Rubel, David. *Scholastic Encyclopedia of the Presidents and Their Times*. New York: Scholastic, 1994.

Schlesinger, Arthur M. Jr. ed. *The Election of 1896 and the Administration of William McKinley*. Philadelphia: Mason Crest Publishers, 2003.

Somerlott, Robert. *The Spanish-American War: Remember the Maine!* Berkeley Heights, NJ: Enslow Publishers, 2002.

The Spanish-American War Centennial Website
http://www.spanamwar.com
This website features numerous articles and links related to the Spanish-American War.

The White House: The Presidents of the United States: Biography of William McKinley
http://www.whitehouse.gov/history/presidents/wm25.html
Read a brief biography of William McKinley from the White House website.

The William McKinley Presidential Library and Museum.
www.mckinleymuseum.org
This website contains information about the McKinley National Memorial and a research center with information about McKinley's personal and professional life.

Wilson, Antoine. *The Assassination of William McKinley*. New York: Rosen Publishing Group, 2002.

Wisconsin War Letters: Spanish-American War: Timeline.
http://www.uwm.edu/Library/arch/Warletters/spanam/SAtimeline
.htm
Visit this page to find links to letters written by Wisconsin soldiers and sailors serving in the Spanish-American War.

The World of 1898: The Spanish-American War
http://www.loc.gov/rr/hispanic/1898
Learn more about the Spanish-American War from the Library of Congress website.

Wukovits, John F. *The Spanish-American War*. San Diego, CA: Lucent Books, 2002.

INDEX

ABOUT THE AUTHOR

Laura B. Edge was born in Waukegan, Illinois, and graduated from the University of Texas at Austin. She went on to study at the American Institute of Foreign Study in London, Paris, Rome, and Athens. Laura has taught reading and writing in elementary schools, middle schools, and at a community college. In addition to teaching, Laura has worked as a computer programmer and has owned and operated a computer training company. She is the author of *Andrew Carnegie: Industrial Philanthropist* and *A Personal Tour of Hull-House*. Laura lives in Kingwood, Texas, with her husband and two sons.

PHOTO ACKNOWLEDGMENTS

The images in this book are used with the permission of: The White House, pp. 1, 7, 10, 19, 27, 37, 47, 58, 68, 78, 89; Library of Congress, pp. 2 (LC-USZ62-117982), 24 (LC-DIG-cwpbh-03770), 34 (LC-USZ62-119055), 36 (LC-USZ62-132536), 43 (LC-USZ62-68573), 55 (LC-USZ62-103205), 59 (LC-USZ62-105073), 60 (LC-USZ62-96543), 64 (LC-USZ62-80), 70 (LC-USZ62-90805), 71 (LC-USZ62-119355), 85 (LC-USZ62-92800), 86 (LC-USZC2-6259), 88 (LC-USZ62-60839), 90 (LC-USZ62-120115), 92 (LC-USZ62-93530), 93 (LC-USZ62-103571), 94 (LC-USZ62-5377), 95 (LC-USZ62-96529); © Brown Brothers, pp. 6, 12 (both), 15, 25, 26, 31, 32, 46, 56, 84, 87; McKinley Memorial Library and Museum, Niles, Ohio, pp. 11, 16, 66, 77, 96; Used by permission from The Wm McKinley Presidential Library and Museum, Canton, Ohio, pp. 18, 42; Rutherford B. Hayes Presidential Center, p. 21; © David J. & Janice L. Frent Collection/CORBIS, p. 30; Ohio Historical Society, p. 48; © Kean Collection/Hulton Archive/Getty Images, p. 52; © Ron Bell Digital Cartographics, p. 61; © Hulton Archive/Getty Images, pp. 63, 80; XNR Productions, p. 69; © Ernest H. Mills/Hulton Archive/Getty Images, p. 73; © Laura Westlund/Independent Picture Service, p. 79; © North Wind Picture Archives, p. 82.

Front Cover: Library of Congress (LC-USZ62-8198).